Runabout Renovation

How to Find and Fix Up an Old Fiberglass Speedboat

Jim Anderson

International Marine
Camden, Maine

International Marine/
Ragged Mountain Press
A Division of The McGraw-Hill Companies

20 19 18 17 16 15 14

Library of Congress Cataloging-in-Publication Data

Anderson, Jim, 1947 Mar. 9-
        Runabout renovation : how to find and fix up an old fiberglass
    speedboat / Jim Anderson.
            p.   cm.
        Includes index.
        ISBN 0-07-158008-5 (formerly 0-87742-295-8)
        1. Fiberglass boats—Maintenance and repair.   2. Motorboats—
    Maintenance and repair.   I. Title.
        VM322.A53   1992
        623.8'231—dc20   91–43505
                                                                         CIP

Questions regarding the content of this book should be addressed to:
International Marine
P.O. Box 220
Camden, ME 04843

Questions regarding the ordering of this book should be addressed to:
The McGraw-Hill Companies
Customer Service Department
P.O. Box 547
Blacklick, OH 43004
Retail customers: 1-800-262-4729
Bookstores: 1-800-722-4726

Runabout Renovation is printed on acid-free paper.
Line illustrations by Rob Groves.
Text design by Rita Naughton.
Typeset by A & B Typesetters, Bow, NH.
Printed by Quebecor Printing, Fairfield, PA.
Edited by Jim Babb and Pamela Benner.
Production by Molly Mulhern.

Contents

————

Acknowledgments

Yor only have to know me to know that this book was not a one-man effort. There are many to whom I owe my deepest appreciation: Tom Frank, friend and computer wizard, was responsible for making sense of my doodlings and providing the artists with understandable line drawings.

Dan Lein, another friend and computer wizard, who became a living manual for my software and hardware because I often failed to comprehend the written material.

Bill Hokness, another friend and shutterbug extraordinaire. He took me by the hand and taught me a bit about how to use a camera.

Mr. Jim Gustner of the Larson Boat company in Little Falls, Minnesota, and Mr. Ron Symanitz of R & R Marine in Shakopee, Minnesota. Both allowed me to roam freely through their facilities with camera in hand.

Last but not least, Jim Babb, my very own editor. Nice goin', coach.

Preface

I began messing about in boats at the tender age of eight, and have since owned about 25 different ones—power, sail, and a few not easily labeled. I have hunted ducks from 12-footers, fished from nearly every type of small craft imaginable, and sailed offshore extensively in sailboats to 57 feet. I maintained most of those boats myself—and learned many repair lessons the hard way.

For several years I applied that accumulated knowledge to the operation of a boat repair shop in southern Minnesota, specializing in restoring and repairing average fiberglass runabouts. My customers were people like myself who had many questions about how to restore or repair their pride and joy. Unfortunately, finding adequate answers was often difficult or impossible. Although more people own boats ranging from 14 to 24 feet than all others combined, most (if not all) published information about boat repair and restoration is directed at the ''big boat'' owner. In addition, many marine dealers and others in the industry seem to have neither the right answers nor the time to spend on us ''little guys.'' Hence this book.

In it, I'll try to guide you through the process of finding, purchasing, and completely renovating the right used boat for your tastes, needs, and pocketbook. Although as an example I have focused on renovating a typical 16-foot fiberglass boat from the early 1970s, the information is sufficiently generic to apply to just about any fiberglass boat under 24 feet you're likely to encounter. That includes those of you who currently own boats in need of repair. For the same reason, and because rotten floors are not unique to fiberglass boats, I also offer tips on renovating an aluminum boat—of which there are many around.

It will soon become evident that I express my opinions freely. Keep in mind that my opinions are simply that; it is not my intent to offend the marine industry or the reader or convert them to my way of thinking. I simply believe that this book's value would be compromised if I withheld my opinions. And I certainly don't mean to imply that I have all the answers on the subject of boat repair. Many of my methods have been developed through the age-old process of trial and error. Others may do things differently, but these techniques have worked for me, and they'll work for you, too.

Before we get started, I think a short story with a message is in order. Several years back a fellow walked into my shop and asked me to take a look at a boat he had in the back of his pickup. As we approached, I couldn't take my eyes off the 5 feet of boat extending from his truck box. I didn't know what it was, but I knew instantly I was in love.

It was a 13-foot duck boat, built of cedar back in the early 1940s, with the most beautiful lines of any boat I'd ever seen. She could have been a battleship.

The fellow that brought it in also loved the boat, but it was in sad shape and he had no idea how to repair it. Rot had taken its toll in several areas, nearly half the oak ribs needed to be replaced, and the entire boat needed to be refitted.

It took only a glance for me to realize that at a shop rate of $38 an hour this guy would be better off buying a new 18-footer. Still, I wanted to take a closer look at that boat, so I told him to leave it; when I could find time I'd take a look at it and see if I couldn't come up with some ideas or suggestions to save her.

We carried it into the shop and set it across a couple of sawhorses in the corner, where it sat for several weeks. Every time I poured a cup of coffee, I found myself leaning on that little boat, wondering how to save it. I was smitten.

Conventional restoration with clear cedar planks and steam-bent oak ribs would have been nearly impossible—and certainly cost prohibitive. I considered taking a fiberglass mold from the hull and building a new boat out of glass, but decided against it. After all, that wasn't really a restoration project anymore, but a completely new boat. Ultimately, I decided that the only way to salvage the original design was to dig out the rot and fiberglass the entire boat.

When the owner came back we discussed his options and, as I expected, he decided he wasn't up to the task of restoring it himself, nor could he justify the expense of having me do it. Naturally, I asked him what he'd take for it. "One hundred dollars," he said. "Are you nuts?" I said. "It's not worth ten." He had me pegged, though. He ended up with the hundred, and I ended up with the boat.

There are two quick lessons here: One, if you're the type who becomes emotional over boats, don't let your enthusiasm cloud your economic judgment. Two, there are better ways to make a living than repairing boats.

I spent months of my spare time on that little boat—filling, sanding, fairing, and repeating the process over and over again. I built solid mahogany seats and side panels for the interior. I painted the hull and deck with $90-a-quart Awlgrip. I installed a battery under the foredeck to operate the new running lights, and cut a custom carpet for the deck. Once completed, she was a proud and beautiful little craft that gave me many pleasurable hours.

For a couple of years I pulled it to boat shows to demonstrate what could be accomplished with a little effort. Everyone who saw it wanted it, but nobody could afford it. Eventually I sold it at a tremendous loss to a fellow I thought would appreciate it.

As promised, there is a lesson here. Some of you may be interested in purchasing and restoring an old boat to save money. After all, you can get on the water for 50 to 70 percent less than the cost of a new boat. Others, like myself, undertake a restoration project simply because it's truly enjoyable and rewarding. But make no mistake, much of the process is just so much hard, dirty work. You may find yourself, during an hour-long attempt to wash away an accumulation of fiberglass dust, wondering *why*.

"Why?" is never an easy question to answer, but the fact that you felt strongly enough about undertaking such a project to purchase this book indicates, to me, that you have a certain relationship with the water and watercraft. I guarantee that if you undertake the project *and finish it*, there will be no prouder skipper on the water. Anywhere.

Good luck,

Jim Anderson

Jim Anderson
Mankato, Minnesota
January 1992

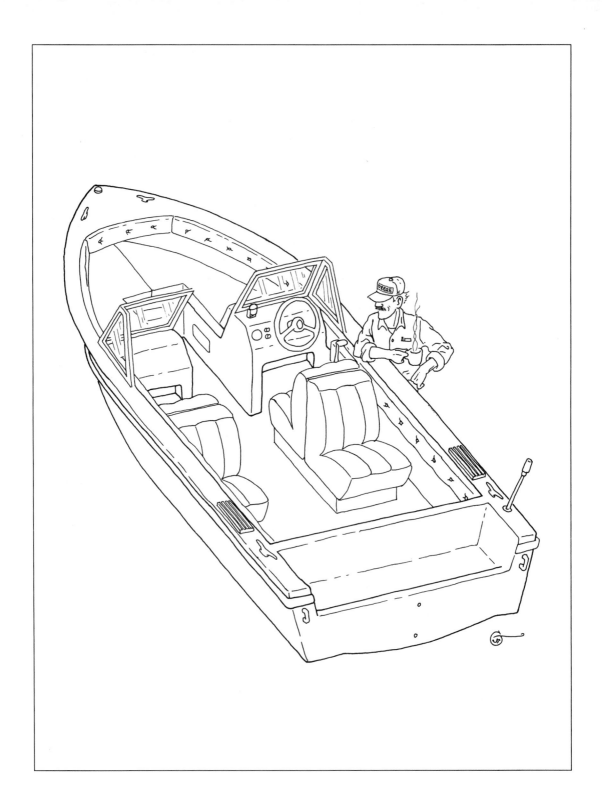

The Birth and Evolution of the Runabout

Trying to determine when the first fiberglass runabout was built is a little like trying to determine when the yam entered the food chain. No one really knows for sure, and neither was accepted that quickly. Fiberglass entered the boatbuilding industry through the slow process of technological evolution. As with any pioneering effort with a new material, many designs and construction methods were tried. Some worked, some didn't.

For centuries prior to the advent of fiberglass, wood had been *the* boatbuilding material. But each boat required hundreds of man-hours by skilled craftsmen, and the high-quality materials necessary for long-lived boats were becoming increasingly scarce and expensive. In the 1940s, many U.S. companies were involved in the research and development of a new wonder material, *fiber-reinforced plastic* (FRP). The Owens-Corning Corporation emerged as the clear front-runner in the early 1950s with the creation of their trademark product, "Fiberglas." Their intensive promotion and marketing was largely responsible for introducing the new technology into the boating industry.

It was then up to the marine industry, anxious to meet expanding demand for recreational watercraft in the booming postwar years, to develop practical applications for the new product. One of their first attempts, in the early 1950s, involved covering conventional wooden hulls with a thin fiberglass shell. This took advantage of the watertight characteristics of fiberglass, but mostly ignored its added strength and durability. More important, it did little to reduce the long and expensive hours of maintenance necessary to keep a wooden boat looking spiffy. It did accomplish one thing, though: It whetted the boat-buying public's appetite for sleeker, faster boats that required less maintenance.

Builders responded quickly, and by the mid-1950s the first solid fiberglass hulls and decks began to appear in showrooms. One of the early successes was the Larson Boat Company and its popular Falls Flyer and Play-Boy models. Today the Falls Flyer is considered a classic; a nicely restored one may sell for $4,000 or more.

Although technology was advancing rapidly, early fiberglass boats were plagued with design and construction flaws. Boats of this era had little freeboard and flat bottoms, which made them exciting to say the least. The Falls Flyer, for example, has been known to roll over on short, fast turns. The fledgling industry, with few guidelines or regulations as to horsepower rating, flotation, or structural engineering, faced monumental problems.

Despite the mistakes, these early designs led a revolution in the boating industry. Suddenly boatbuilders had at their disposal a composite material that could be sprayed and molded into a boat by semiskilled labor in a fraction of the time required for a wooden boat to be laboriously constructed, piece by piece, by artisans. Molded fiberglass boats made possible the dream of an affordable, easily maintained, well-performing boat for Everyman.

How Fiberglass Boats Are Built

Mass-produced fiberglass boats are pulled, one after the other, from *molds*—a female impression of the hull or deck. Molds are formed over *plugs*—essentially a wooden replica of the finished boat. The mold and the hull are both laid up from alternating layers of fiberglass materials woven either into *cloth* or *roving*, both of which provide lateral strength, or compressed into *mat*, which provides cohesion and builds up thickness. The glass material is saturated with *polyester resin*, which cures rock-hard. The hull's outer layer is a form of resin known as *gelcoat*, which provides the color, high gloss, and durable finish you see in the showroom. In some high-tech operations, the alternating layers of mat and resin may be sprayed into place using mixing devices called *chopper guns*.

This is not as complicated as it sounds. Let's assume that you want to create an exact replica of your child's toy boat. The hard part has already been done; the toy boat's hull forms the plug. Set that hull into wet plaster and allow it to dry, and you have a female mold. Now lay up layers of resin-saturated fiberglass material inside the mold. When it cures or hardens, you have a fiberglass reproduction of the toy boat.

Once a builder settles on a design, a plug is built of wood, much like a wooden boat. Joints and surface flaws are carefully filled, then the plug is ground, sanded, and faired. Any imperfections will be transferred to the mold and in turn to the actual hull, so the plug must be flawless.

Next, to allow the cured mold to be removed, the plug is waxed or coated with a releasing agent, then sprayed with polyester resin and subsequent layers of chopped fiberglass to form the mold. A tubular steel or wood frame is built around the mold to retain its shape, then the female mold is pulled from the plug. By reversing the process the actual hull can now be formed inside the female mold.

The layup process varies from builder to builder and design to design, but virtually all builders begin the layup process by first spraying a layer of polyester gelcoat inside the mold. Next come alternating layers of glass cloth, woven roving, and mat until the desired hull thickness is achieved. Each layer is saturated with polyester resin as it is applied. When the resin cures, the result is a laminated hull that is extremely durable. (In fact, it is nearly indestructible. Florida, for instance, currently is in a quandary about how to dispose of all its derelict fiberglass hulls. Because of environmental considerations they cannot be burned, buried, or sunk.) Once the hull has been removed from the mold it enters the assembly line,

Figure 1-1. Producing fiberglass boats.

Step 1: The process begins with a wooden replica of the boat, the plug.

Step 2: The plug is sprayed with layers of chopped fiberglass to form the mold.

Step 3: The hull is formed inside the mold from layers of glass fiber and polyester. Note the high gloss of the finished mold.

Step 4: The layup process begins with a layer of gelcoat followed by alternating layers of glass cloth, woven roving, or mat. Each layer is saturated with polyester resin; the whole club-sandwich–like mess cures into a durable fiberglass hull.

Step 5: The deck section is constructed just as the hull is, on a separate assembly line. Note that the instrument panel, splash well, and other accoutrements are already in place.

where it is fitted with stringers, frames, flotation, the floor, bilge pumps and the like, and the wooden transom.

Meanwhile, on a separate assembly line, a matching deck section has been built in an identical process. The deck section is fitted with the helm station, wiring harness, deck hardware, instruments, seat bases, and related equipment. The final step in the boat's assembly occurs when the two sections meet at the end of the assembly line, where they are attached and the finishing touches added.

Of course the complete process of building a fiberglass runabout is much more complex that what I've outlined, but then I'm not trying to put anyone in the boatbuilding business. All you really need for now is a basic understanding of how the boats are built. As the need arises, we'll examine specific construction methods more closely.

Designs

While builders were busy developing new construction methods from scratch, they were also faced with developing designs that appealed to an eager new market, much of which owed no allegiance to and had no love for traditional naval architecture.

The low freeboard and flat bottoms of the early models were quickly replaced by deeper V-hulls, which eliminated many of the handling problems. The V-hull also gave a quieter, safer, and more comfortable ride, which was substantially enhanced by the boat's weight. This was when American industry seemed to overbuild everything. Our automobiles were made of real steel and lots of it. That same more-is-better philosophy also applied to the fiberglass boats of the 1960s and early 1970s. The comparison between boats and automobiles didn't stop at weight, either. The car-like boats of the late 1950s and early 1960s were all but indistinguishable from the boat-like cars: the steering wheels and dashboards were a near match; pleated upholstery was everywhere; and fins were in.

Although the V-hull was a vast improvement over the first flat-bottomed efforts and provided a sound basic design from which to experiment, its execution left much to be desired. Again, in an attempt to be as car-like as possible, a typical 16-foot boat might have nearly a third of its length covered by a long, hood-like deck—usually topped by an oversize windshield, which made it difficult to move forward when docking or beaching. The space under the deck was good only for storage and severely limited room for passengers.

Figure 1-2. A V-hull runabout is very stable in heavy seas, but early models didn't allow access forward.

To make use of this wasted area in the bow, designers in the late 1960s and early 1970s came up with the *walk-through*, or *bow-rider*, which had a seating area forward of the control console. Although I can't find anyone to confirm this, I suspect that, now that the boat's extreme bow could be occupied by passengers, designers felt it necessary to add stability forward by widening the bow. At any rate, simultaneous with the appearance of the walk-through came the *tri-hull*.

All the added interior space made the tri-hulls immediately popular, but new design problems surfaced, most noticeably in the ride. Unlike the V-hulls, which cut through waves, the tri-hulls tended to slap over them, resulting in a much rougher ride. The constant pounding at high speed also caused windshield hardware, electrical connections, seat hardware, etc. to work loose. The tri-hulls may have been stable in calm water, but when things got a little sloppy they proved difficult to handle. In heavy seas, some of the early models were downright unsafe.

Over the years many companies experimented with the basic tri-hull

Figure 1-3.   A tri-hull runabout with an open bow allows access forward at the cost of a rough ride in choppy water.

design, and it has been extensively modified to attempt to minimize its drawbacks. However, except for a few notable exceptions, such as the Boston Whaler, tri-hulls have not stood the test of time, and today new boats with the traditional tri-hull are hard to find.

Today's showrooms are filled with a new generation of runabouts often referred to as *fish-and-skis*, which combine the comfort, safety, and inherent stability of the V-hull with an open bow previously found only in tri-hulls. These boats are available with a wide array of accessories—removable pedestal seats, live wells, extra power—and appeal to a wide variety of boaters.

Finding the Right Boat

There are two broad rules to follow when thinking about a suitable candidate for your first renovation project (those of you who may have a boat already, read on: much of this applies to you, too). First, unless you have a professional workspace, tools, and knowledge, avoid any boat with severe structural damage to the hull or deck. You'll simply spend too much time and money on the restoration; besides, there are too many good used boats available to put yourself through the pain of trying to restore a wreck.

Second, try to stick with boats from a proven builder. Builders don't stay in business for 20 or 30 years by building bad boats. Most reputable builders are perfectly happy to offer advice to people restoring one of their boats, and usually can supply unique parts that might otherwise be impossible to obtain.

As with most rules there are exceptions, however. Some very reputable builders of today built some real lemons in their early years. For example, I've replaced floors in Glastrons that were only six years old; also, in my opinion there was insufficient fiberglass in the sides of their hulls. At one time, Forester completely filled the hull below floor level with foam. The result was a floor predestined to rot, and one that was extremely difficult to replace once this happened.

When you have spotted a likely prospect, give it a proper survey (covered in the next chapter), then research the builder by contacting dealers and repair shops in your area. Ask them to give you any information they can about the boat and its builder. Builders come and go, and molds are bought and sold. The boat you have chosen may be in production under a different name.

Also keep in mind that many builders of the 1960s were regional. Just because a name is unfamiliar doesn't mean it isn't a good boat. Freight costs often prohibited builders from competing outside their immediate area. I have seen many good boats of this vintage come through my shop that I had never heard of here in the Midwest, although they may have been very popular elsewhere. Again, do your research, but before you set off in search of the perfect restoration prospect, here are a few additional things to consider:

❑ Give careful thought to how the boat will be used *most* of the time. If you'll be spending the bulk of your time fishing in coastal waters or one of the Great Lakes, look for a heavy V-hull that will provide you with a safe and comfortable ride.

❑ An old, open-bow tri-hull isn't really a safe and comfortable rough-water boat, but in more sheltered waters it can be perfectly suitable. The open bow provides extra interior space—good for fishing or quiet cruising on a Sunday afternoon. Properly powered, a tri-hull will easily pull a tube, knee board, or water-skier.

❑ An obvious consideration is your budget. Generally speaking, the older the boat the less you can expect to pay. Keep in mind that polyester resin is a petroleum by-product. As a rule, boats built before the oil embargo of the early 1970s generally have more glass and resin in their construction. Once restored, they'll last forever.

❑ Remember that the glut of used boats of this type make this a buyer's market. There is simply no need to accept the bottom line from a stubborn seller. Chances are you'll find an identical boat sitting in the corner of some yard not far from home.

❑ There is little difference between the price of a V-hull or a tri-hull of the same year. In most areas you should be able to buy either one, sitting on a trailer, for $500 or less.

❑ A V-hull with a closed bow usually will be the least expensive to restore if the upholstery needs replacing; open-bow tri-hulls simply have more cushions. Otherwise, the cost to restore a V-hull or a tri-hull of the same size will be about the same.

❑ If you are a bass fisherman who plans to spend the bulk of your time in quiet backwaters casting for a state record, you may want to look for a bassboat, but give the purchase some additional thought. Bassboats are relatively new on the scene, which means that one in decent shape is likely to cost considerably more than an older V-hull or tri-hull. The race to capture the bassboat market followed somewhat the same path as the evolution of the fiberglass runabout. While builders experimented with this new and unique design, some junk got built. Some used balsa-cored hulls, which are tricky to build in small sizes and often have internal rot problems that are difficult to spot. Few builders anticipated the huge outboards that would find their way onto the back of a typical bassboat, and as a result many of the early transoms were inadequate. Bassboats also seemed to run to metalflake gelcoats. Personally, I don't care for metalflake finishes on any boat, and I assure you that on a used boat (or new, for that matter) they will cause you problems, unless you faithfully cover the boat with a tarp. Restoring a bassboat will also cost considerably more than restoring a tri-hull or V-hull. They leave the factory with all the bells and whistles, and many will have to be replaced. Some have two live-well pumps that may cost $40 each to replace. Each pump has its own hose and through-hull fitting, which will probably be brittle and need replacing. A simple switch may cost $10. Early pedestal seats used aluminum pedestals set directly into aluminum bases. You can bet they're worn out.

I'll say it one more time: Research and a proper survey are the keys to avoiding a bad experience. I've had many boats come into my shop that had been half restored by folks who ran into surprises.

Where To Look, and How To Drive a Bargain

With the exception of putting the finished product in the water for the first time, looking for the right boat is the most enjoyable aspect of a runabout renovation project. I don't know a single confirmed boat freak who doesn't thoroughly enjoy wandering through boatyards and crawling around, under, and through boats. It's one of those few cheap pastimes you can do most anywhere.

Start your search with newspapers and shopper and trading magazines in your area. In my experience, two types of sellers use this media to sell their boat: One is sick of having the thing sitting around, and he'll take whatever he can get just so he can mow under it. The other has decided it's time for a new boat and needs the cash for a down payment, but he's often emotionally attached to his old tub and asking twice what it's worth.

The fact that these sellers have invested money in advertising indicates they are motivated to sell, but it also means you may be able to save 10 or 20 percent somewhere else from someone who *hasn't* invested money in advertising. Something to bear in mind. In any event, give them a call and get the particulars on the boat and the asking price—which may be as much as 50 percent more than what you want to spend. If it sounds interesting, though, go take a look.

Give the boat a proper survey (see Chapter 2) and point out its faults. If the owner begins to look uncertain, make an offer based not on the asking price, but on what you can afford. All he can say is "no." If he does, leave him your phone number and tell him to give you a call if he changes his mind. After he's spent another hundred bucks on advertising, your phone may ring.

You can often find a real steal in the want ads, but you'll probably invest some time and gas checking them out. With that in mind, don't ignore local dealers. Most have a lot full of trade-ins they would love to sell. In addition, boats of this vintage (1960s to early 1970s) are generally considered junk by new boat dealers, and they seldom have little if any hard cash invested in the trade-in. Today, few manufacturers offer their dealers more than a 25 percent profit margin on new boats. To be competitive, many dealers must give away 10 to 15 percent on a cash deal. In many cases, when the dealer is confronted with a trade-in he'll give the buyer the same 10 to 15 percent, meaning he has virtually nothing invested in the trade-in. He has already made what he expects to make on a new cash sale, and now he has this junker taking up space in his yard.

Naturally, he'll try to get as much for the used boat as he can. After all, anything he gets can be considered 100 percent profit. But the right boat—at least from your viewpoint; the dealer is apt to consider it anything *but* the right boat—sitting in an overcrowded yard will usually go cheap, cheap, cheap. Again, survey the boat well and don't be afraid to make what might be considered an insulting offer. Even a dealer may be unaware of hidden problems. If you point them out, you may get a real buy.

I can't think of a better way to spend a Saturday afternoon than walking through marinas looking for "FOR SALE" signs. You'll be dealing with private owners, and since the boat is probably sitting in or near the water, you may be able to take it for a test ride. The fact that the boat's in use may also indicate that it's in relatively good condition. Don't take it for granted, though. Follow the rules and give the boat a proper survey.

Within the past several years a new outlet has been created for sellers who wish to sell their boats with a no-muss, no-fuss approach. Many dealers with ample yard space will now take boats in the runabout class on consignment, which is not to be confused with brokerage. Traditionally, the brokerage of boats has been restricted to larger boats with higher sticker prices. The broker and the seller sign a formal contract that gives the broker a commission, usually 10 percent, on the boat's final sale price. Someone trying to sell his $1,500 runabout is probably not too wild about giving a broker 10 percent of his boat's ultimate selling price.

The consignment agreement between a seller and a dealer is much more versatile than formal brokerage. Usually, the seller establishes a bottom dollar that he will accept and agrees that the dealer will take everything he can get over that amount.

For instance, if I take my boat to a consignment dealer and tell him that I won't accept less than $1,500, the dealer can put it on his lot for whatever price he thinks the market will bear. Let's assume he starts high, asking, say, $2,200. If you, the smart buyer, walk in a week later and offer the dealer a fair price of $1,600, he has two options: He can take his $100 profit for having the boat on his lot for one week, or he can call me up and try to talk me into taking less than the original $1,500 I wanted. In either case, the smart buyer wins.

What if the boat has been sitting in the same lot for a year and a half? The canvas, upholstery, and carpet are beginning to show neglect; the gelcoat is fading; and the boat is full of leaves. The seller is wondering if he will ever sell that albatross, and the dealer is sick of looking at it.

You, the smart buyer, walk in and offer $800 for the boat. It's entirely possible that the dealer will run to the phone, call the seller, and talk him into taking $700, leaving the dealer with $100. You win again.

The advantage of the consignment lot is that the seller is usually motivated. He doesn't want to invest any cash in advertising, nor does he want the hassle of showing the boat to prospective buyers. In most cases he simply wants to rid himself of the boat as simply and painlessly as possible.

One final suggestion. While you're driving between boatyards, marinas, and the homes of advertisers, keep your eyes open. In my part of the country, some of the best buys can be found sitting in the backyards, groves, or sheds of sellers who have given up trying to sell their boats. Maybe the boat has a cottonwood tree growing out of the floor, but go take a look anyway. If the hull and deck are sound, it may be just what you're looking for.

A SMART SHOPPER'S CHECKLIST

❑ Consider carefully how you'll use the boat *most* of the time.

❑ Decide how much you can afford and stick to it.

❑ Don't buy an obvious junker.

❑ Stick to a proven builder.

❑ Give every boat a proper survey (see Chapter 2).

❑ Find out what you can about the builder and the availability of unique parts (windshields, rail extrusions, etc.).

❑ Estimate repairs and deduct the cost from the total you want to spend.

❑ Spend plenty of time looking for the right boat, and keep notes on your survey and cost of repairs.

❑ When you've found what you want, tell the owner about needed repairs, then BARGAIN!

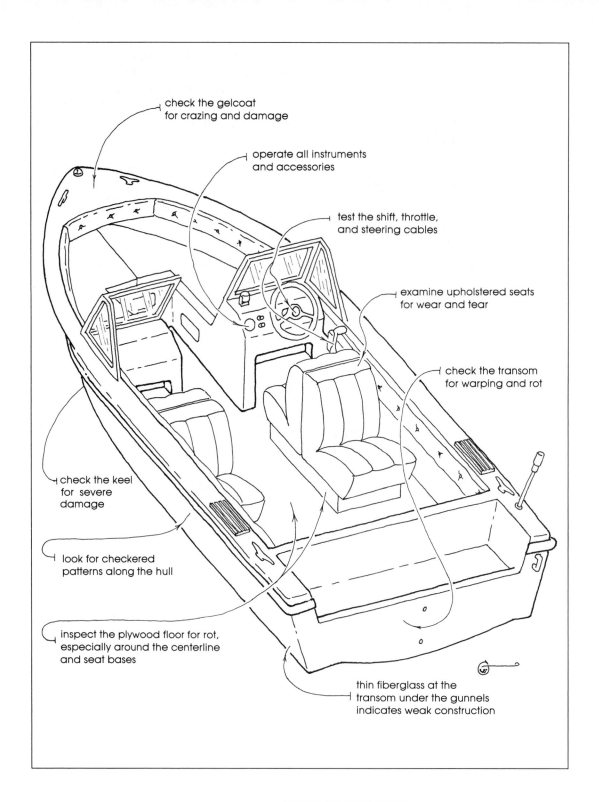

check the gelcoat
for crazing and damage

operate all instruments
and accessories

test the shift, throttle,
and steering cables

examine upholstered seats
for wear and tear

check the transom
for warping and rot

check the keel
for severe
damage

look for checkered
patterns along the hull

inspect the plywood floor for rot,
especially around the centerline
and seat bases

thin fiberglass at the
transom under the gunnels
indicates weak construction

CHAPTER

2

The Dark Art
of Surveying

———

In 1988, while sailing along the west
coast of Florida, I discovered the boat of my dreams, and it just happened
to be for sale. It was a 38-foot, full-keel ketch, typically Taiwanese and
loaded with teak. Although it had been sadly neglected for several years, I
spotted a beautiful boat beneath the cosmetic shortcomings, one that
could be bought *cheap*. Unfortunately it was the final day of my vacation, and I only had time to obtain an equipment list and asking price
from the broker, who also supplied me with the names of several local
surveyors.

After returning to Minnesota I studied the equipment list, researched
the boat, and ultimately made an offer about 30 percent lower than the
owner's asking price. He accepted without a counterproposal, which
means I probably offered too much. I knew I could fix the cosmetic problems myself, and my research made me reasonably certain of its sailing
characteristics, but without an in-depth inspection I had no idea of the
boat's true overall condition.

I arbitrarily phoned a surveyor from the broker's list, he sent a substantial list of most impressive credentials, and I hired him. Several days
later I received his survey. Beyond the obvious cosmetic problems and a
stuffing box that needed repacking, he had found no serious problems.
All things considered, it was a good survey with no expensive surprises,
not even the reasonable invoice of $300.

I called the broker, made arrangements to sleep on the boat for a few days, then headed back to Florida to look over the boat more closely and get local estimates for obvious repairs and upgrades. By the time I was finished I had a fair idea what it would take to make her shipshape.

Still trusting in the survey and expecting no serious problems, a friend and I went for a test sail with the owner. With him at the helm, we exited the canal and made ready to hoist the sails. I was more excited than on the day I got my first bike.

The first thing I noticed when I removed the sail cover was several small holes in the mainsail and a 2- to 3-inch bow in the spruce boom. Mainsails and spruce booms are expensive, but the surveyor had not listed them as substandard. Both problems were so obvious that it seemed unlikely he had ever taken the sail cover off the boom. So much for the excitement of a new bike. I began to wonder what else he had missed.

To make a long story short, I found many other obvious problems, including a rotten deck core. My dream boat had turned into an expensive nightmare. That was my first and last experience with a "professional" surveyor, and the lessons I learned are not unique to the purchase of a big boat.

Obviously, surveying the typical runabout is far less complex than surveying a 38-footer, but all things being relative, the emotional and financial impact of a poor choice can be just as disastrous.

Educate Yourself

You probably won't depend on the credentials of an out-of-state surveyor when purchasing your runabout. You'll have to be comfortable with making the final analysis yourself—and there is much you'll need to know. There are many 16-foot fiberglass flowerpots sitting in the backyards of complacent buyers.

If you've read this far you should have a fairly good idea what you're looking for in terms of hull and interior design, make, and vintage. You may also have some idea of the kinds of cosmetic and structural problems you might find. Of course it's of little use to understand what problems may exist unless you know how to recognize them. And the best way to learn to recognize them is to spend as much time as you can crawling over, under, and through as many different kinds of boats as you can find. Besides, it's just plain fun. And the education gained won't be beneficial just to someone out shopping for a used boat. Those who currently own an older boat will find it helpful in creating preventive maintenance schedules and making tough decisions about repairing or trading.

As stated in Chapter 1, unless you have extensive experience in fiberglass repair, avoid boats with obvious and severe hull or deck damage. These will be just too complex and expensive to repair or restore. Besides, there are too many *good* used boats available to warrant the risk.

Obvious damage aside, don't be overly concerned with a boat's initial appearance. Keep in mind that we're looking for a steal, and the seller is already aware of the cosmetic problems. If you can point out more serious problems, you may be on your way to buying your boat for pocket change.

Unless the boat is in current use, and thus receiving periodic care, you can expect the gelcoat to have little or no shine left. That lack of luster will be especially noticeable on horizontal deck surfaces directly exposed to the sun's ultraviolet rays. It will be even more evident on those decks with colored gelcoat. The deck in Figure 2-1 is (or was) red.

Figure 2-1. Your renovation project almost certainly will include restoring a dull gelcoat, particularly if your runabout has a colored deck.

The reds, blues, and black seem to fade more dramatically than lighter colors. You can restore darker colors with rubbing compound and multiple coats of a good marine wax, but only to a point. Depending on the sun's intensity in your area, a dark pigment may have to be rubbed out twice a year. In fact, it is possible to *destroy* the gelcoat with excessive use of rubbing compound, leaving a complete paint job as the only practical and cost-effective repair. Although this book assumes a total renovation, if you want to avoid painting the boat I suggest you avoid colored decks. A white deck is far easier to restore and maintain than colored gelcoats. If you purchase a boat with colored decks in relatively good condition, keep a tarp on it when not in use or eventually it will fade.

The same applies to many metalflake finishes. In extreme cases of deterioration you can actually feel the metal flakes poking through the gelcoat. At best these finishes demand a maintenance-conscious owner who will keep the boat covered when not in use. Inspect all such finishes carefully.

Close inspection of the gelcoat will likely reveal a phenomenon known as *crazing*. This may show up anywhere on the hull or deck as a series of hairline cracks radiating outward from a center point. They often

Figure 2-2. You'll want to avoid boats with significant crazing. The case shown here isn't too bad and is relatively easy to repair. If your proposed renovator looks like a moonscape, though, walk the other way.

remind me of a daddy longlegs. There is much speculation about what causes these unsightly little cracks. Some contend that they result from flexing, perhaps caused by direct impact. Others suggest that they occur when the hull or deck section is removed from the mold. Yet others speculate that it is caused by the chemical breakdown of a given batch of resin. Crazing may also result from a gelcoat that has become brittle because it was applied too thickly. All of these things may contribute to crazing, but I prefer to classify them simply as phenomena—minor mysteries to science and pains in the neck to the boat painter.

Crazing poses no threat to the boat's structural integrity, but if you're planning to paint your boat any color other than the original, it will cause you problems: Crazed areas simply will not accept paint. The smallest cracks can be filled with a sandable primer, but most will survive the best preparation and prime job. If your new paint is darker than the original gelcoat, the lighter-colored cracks will be very noticeable.

I've seen boats literally covered with crazing, and my only suggestion is to avoid those boats unless you're prepared to live with the cracks. On the other hand, I've seen few boats of this vintage that didn't have at least a few bad spots, so in Chapter 6 I discuss a couple of methods to repair the worst areas.

The Hull

A solidly built fiberglass boat will appear bulky, with a rounded bow stem and decklines; fiberglass was never intended to make sharp corners. If you poke around in enough boatyards and look at enough boats, you'll soon learn to recognize the subtle differences in appearance between a well-made boat and one where the builder skimped on materials. There are other indicators of general hull quality.

Stand at the boat's stern and look forward along the sides of the hull. The gelcoat may be dull and scratched, but the finish should be flat and smooth, with no visible pattern. Many builders used woven roving for the first layer of fiberglass. If the gelcoat isn't thick enough, the characteristic basket-weave pattern of the roving will show through the gelcoat. All too often, further inspection will show that a single layer of roving constitutes the only layer of fiberglass used in the sides of the hull. The older Glastrons and many bassboats come to mind. Boats built this way were easily holed above the waterline, and even though they may have survived for 15 years, they aren't the type of hull that you want to invest time and money in restoring.

On certain designs the hull thickness may be evident from the inside, if you can find an area where the vinyl or carpet is loose. Feel under the gunnels at the hull/deck joint. Boats in the 16-foot range seldom have hull sides thicker than ¼ inch. The thicker the better.

At each corner of the stern you'll usually find aluminum corner caps attached with one or two stainless steel screws. Remove the screws and cap. On some designs you'll be able to determine the thickness of the hull side as well as that of the transom. The type of hull/deck joint used also will be evident.

Spend some time pushing on the sides of the boat with your hands. This simple procedure may be the most effective test of hull rigidity. Under pressure, there should be little or no flex in the sides. Press *hard* right under the hull/deck joint, along the entire length of the hull. *Any* flex or separation indicates insufficient hull thickness and/or leaks at the joint. Again, to find a benchmark try flexing different boats until you find one that flexes too easily.

The second area to inspect closely is the bottom of the hull. Because of the floor it will be difficult if not impossible to determine the thickness of the bottom, but in most cases adequate construction in the sides indicates the same in the bottom. Hidden problems in the bottom generally are revealed through a close inspection from the outside.

Gouges and scratches are to be expected, especially along the keel, which is constantly subjected to contact with beaches, trailers, and often rocks. Consider them as normal wear, and plan on repairing them when you paint the boat. However, if the keel shows obvious signs of *severe* damage, the boat is probably not worth your effort.

Pay close attention to any area that looks obviously different, such as dented or bulged areas. These often will have small cracks seeping water or showing recent signs—dirty or rust-colored stains around the cracks— of having been wet. In many cases, discolored cracks indicate a leak. You may even find a single drop of water hanging from a crack several days after the last rain. If this is the case, you can bet that the foam flotation is saturated with water and serving no purpose. Replacing the flotation will mean replacing the floor, regardless of its condition. The leak can be repaired from the inside after the foam has been removed, leaving only a cosmetic repair to be done on the outside. But if you're not up to the entire project, avoid the leaker.

At this point, we'd better briefly discuss cored or *sandwich construction* hulls. A core material, such as foam or end-grain balsa wood (the most common core for boats of this era), is sandwiched between multiple layers of fiberglass to make the boat stiffer and lighter. Balsa core construction is much more common in larger craft because of its superior strength-to-weight ratio over solid fiberglass. However, I have come across balsa cores a few times in boats in the 18- to 20-foot range, and once in a

Figure 2-3. Cored construction. Think Oreos. The goop in the middle that you eat first is, on the boat, either foam or end-grain balsa wood. The other stuff is fiberglass.

16-foot bassboat. On each occasion the boats were suitable only for the scrap pile.

I certainly have no objections to balsa cores, and because of the superior strength-to-weight ratio I expect you'll see an increase in the use of cored hulls in boats of this size. However, if damage to the fiberglass skin allows water to enter in sufficient quantities to saturate the core, sooner or later the skin and core will separate, and the now unsupported skin will become very fragile.

Separation will be evident from bulges or waves in the hull. A gentle push on the high spots will cause them to buckle freely. Even if you've never seen it before, you'll know. In most cases, repair or replacement will be cost prohibitive in boats of this size. Avoid cored hulls unless the hull is in exceptionally good condition. You can find out from the builder whether your prospective renovation candidate has a core, and if so, what type.

The final area of concern is the hull/deck joint. Different types of joints are discussed in Chapter 5. Here we are only concerned with the aluminum extrusion that covers the joint and, to a certain extent, becomes part of the joint's integrity.

It isn't uncommon to find fairly severe damage at the hull/deck joint. Generally, the damage will be forward on either side, often the result of collisions, either with another boat, a day marker (it happens), or more probably with a pesky dock post, which is what happened to the boat in Figure 2-4.

Figure 2-4. Be on the lookout for damaged hull/deck joints, particularly where repairing the aluminum extrusion will be difficult.

Typically, damage to the fiberglass of the hull or deck sections in this area can be repaired easily. Damage to the aluminum extrusion is another story. Inspect it carefully. If it's kinked, dented, or bent to the point that it can't be straightened, finding a replacement can be difficult and expensive. (This also applies to the oddball extrusion, but more on this in Chapter 5.)

If the builder is still in business, they may be able to provide you with a new extrusion, or at least point you in the right direction. Extrusions can be expensive, though, so check the cost of a replacement before buying the boat.

If the boat hasn't been in production for many years, finding a replacement extrusion may require a bit of searching. If your prospect is sitting in a boatyard, begin by checking the boat next door. Most builders in the 1960s and 1970s used only two or three different types of hull/deck joints. Consequently, many extrusions are interchangeable, and you may be able to find a junker boat with an entire piece or a section that may be cut to replace the damaged area.

The problems of finding extrusions may also extend to the transom cap, stern and bow caps, and windshield channels. If these parts are missing, damaged, or of unique design, try to find replacements before closing the deal on your boat.

The Interior

Armed with nothing more than a flashlight and an awl, you should be able to draw accurate conclusions about the overall condition of the boat's interior. This is where you'll find the most time-consuming and expensive repairs, and it is also the one part of the survey that may serve to lower the asking price considerably. The owner is certainly aware of the obvious and visible cosmetic problems and has probably set his asking

Figure 2-5. Bow caps, stern caps, and other aluminum extrusions can be costly or impossible to replace. Check around the boatyard; you may find a derelict with just the extrusion you want.

price accordingly. However, he may not be aware that the boat needs a $500 floor or a $700 transom. Find those problems and point them out. *Then* bargain.

Start by inspecting the upholstery, which will almost certainly need replacing on most boats of this vintage. Unless you're handy with a commercial sewing machine, it may also be one of the most costly repairs you'll encounter; depending on the number of pieces involved, you may spend $200 to $400 on a new suit of upholstery. You can save a lot of money by removing the old upholstery pieces and taking them to the shop to use as patterns. When looking for sewing bids, be sure to make it clear that you will remove the old material from the seats and replace the new ones yourself (details in Chapter 7).

It's a good idea to get an estimate or two for replacing the upholstery before making an offer on a boat. It will give you a better understanding of the overall cost of restoration—and put you in a better bargaining position with the owner.

Seat bottoms, backs, and bases of this era usually are construction-

Figure 2-6. Expect your renovation project to include replacing the upholstery. Sun and suntan lotion ensure its early demise.

grade plywood, and with all the inadequately sealed screws attaching the hardware, they are often rotten (repairs and improvements are discussed in Chapter 7). With your awl, probe the backs and bottoms thoroughly. If you can't yet distinguish between sound and rotten plywood, my only advice is to crawl through more boats, poking away with your awl until you become familiar with the different feel. In short, the awl will penetrate rotten wood with little effort; the more rotten the wood is, the easier the awl penetrates.

When probing the seats or bases, also probe the floor around the seats, which is often one of the first areas to rot. The seats usually are attached to the floor with screws, and inevitably the screws have allowed water to reach the plywood laminates. Rot radiates outward from this area, which means that eventually you'll have to replace the entire floor. However, if the soft spots are limited to a small area, such as around the seats, it means that you have discovered the problem in its early stages, and the stringers and frames probably have not been affected. Either way, the entire floor will have to be replaced to ensure a proper repair.

The Transom

As you probe the floor with your awl, work your way aft and repeat the process on the entire surface of the transom. More than likely, you'll in-

Figure 2-7. When conducting a survey, be particularly suspicious of the floor around seats.

spect the floor carefully because it probably is covered with a vinyl or carpet covering, which may hide visible signs of rot. Don't cheat on the transom simply because it has no similar covering. Generally, transoms of this era were sprayed with resin and chopped fiberglass. Beneath this shiny surface may lurk a rotten plywood transom core. Pay special attention to all hardware mounted into or through the transom, such as outboard mounting bolts, towing eyes, and drain tubes. Often rot will begin around the hardware and spread outward.

There are a few additional areas that may indicate the condition of an outboard boat's transom. Take a look at the legs of the outboard mounting bracket. If the bracket legs have punctured the fiberglass hull, you can be sure the transom core will crumble once exposed. Also, sight along the outside of the transom from corner to corner. Ideally it will be straight, although that is seldom the case. Many builders of this period tended to overestimate their boats' horsepower ratings. Even when the ratings were

Figure 2-8. Study the edge of the transom for an outward bow. It can be pulled back into shape, but it's work.

realistic, many owners just ignored them. Big, powerful outboards are heavy, possess a high degree of torque when pulling up a skier, and all outboards tend to bounce when trailered. Those combined factors often result in an outward bow to the transom and serious stress cracks on the inside corners of the splash well. The stress cracks don't necessarily mean that the transom is rotten, but they may indicate that it is getting soft, and this certainly means that you have a difficult repair to the splash well—one that may require separating the hull and deck sections to gain access to the back of the splash well. If you've gone that far, you may as well replace the transom, too.

There is one final area that may indicate the condition of the transom. When removing the corner cap to inspect the hull thickness, the top edge of the transom may be exposed on some designs. On others, it may be possible to feel the top edge of the transom from inside the boat. Some builders completely sealed the top edge of the transom with resin because they recognized its potential for rot. Many did not. If you can get a look at the top edge of the transom, it should be bright, with all the laminates intact. A dull-gray color and slight delamination don't always indicate a rotten transom, but they do indicate that it has taken in some water. The top edge should be saturated with resin as a preventive measure.

I have not encountered major transom problems in inboard or sterndrive designs. I expect this is due partly to the design itself, which demands more care in construction, and partly to the deck, which efficiently protects the transom. However, because a damaged transom on an inboard or sterndrive boat will be very difficult and expensive to repair, give the whole area a thorough survey.

Hidden Wood

I don't think the average boater is aware of just how much wood is used in fiberglass boat construction. With the exception of stringers and frames, it's all construction-grade plywood—and all subject to rot.

We've already talked about the floor and the transom, and I mentioned earlier that it's also used in seat backs, bottoms, and bases. There's more. Most consoles have a piece of plywood on the back side that serves as backing for mounting instruments. Some designs used upholstered plywood side panels and bulkheads under the consoles. Many builders added a piece of plywood under the gunnels for extra support and for attaching deck hardware. You may find a small strip on the inside of a shoebox hull/deck joint (see Chapter 5 for more on shoebox joints), or under the decks of older V-hulls. Bassboats have a piece glassed to the underside of casting platforms to support pedestal seats and provide purchase for mounting hardware. Occasionally, you'll find plywood storage compartments and rod boxes or lids for live wells.

Some of these applications are more susceptible to rot than others, but a proper survey should include close inspection of all of them. You'll probably find yourself standing on your head and wishing your arm were a foot longer, but a thorough job of checking all these hidden wood parts may prevent some nasty surprises.

Now that you've inspected the gelcoat, interior, hull, floor, transom, and the hidden wood, you should have a fair idea of how extensive your renovation will be. Don't be intimidated by the prospect of replacing the floor or transom. It may be hard work, but the expense is minimal. If the hull and deck are of sound design and in fair to good condition, the remainder of the boat can be completely rebuilt. And remember: Pointing out a rotten floor or transom to the seller can lower a boat's asking price dramatically.

Accessories

My credentials as a mechanic are not impressive, so I'll spend little time discussing engines or outboard motors (if your interest extends to things mechanical and classic, you might want to pick up a copy of *The Old Outboard Book*, International Marine, 1991; for more contemporary powerplants, see *Keep Your Outboard Motor Running* and *Keep Your Sterndrive Running*, International Marine, 1992). If there is an outboard involved in the purchase, it will probably represent a substantial portion of the purchase price and warrant a survey of its own. I suggest you have it tested by a qualified mechanic and, if possible, take it for a test run. However, you need no technical expertise to check the throttle, shift, and steering cables. Operate the throttle and shift controls and turn the wheel in a full sweep several times. Throttle and shift cables are relatively inexpensive; if they are frozen due to age and rust, I wouldn't be overly concerned. On the other hand, a frozen steering cable may run as much as $250 depending on the size of the boat.

If the steering cable moves at all, chances are good that a complete lube job at the motor will restore it to its original ease of operation. If you can't budge it, the cable itself has rusted beyond repair. I've tried several times to free them up with a variety of lubricants with little success. Replacement is the only sure cure.

While examining the throttle and steering cables, take a look at the 12-volt wiring harness. In most cases the wiring harness runs aft from the dash, within the same wire ties as the other cables. If many of the wires are broken or cracked, it is usually easier to rewire the entire boat than to repair or replace selective wires (more on wiring in Chapter 8).

Without taking the boat for a test run, or at least hooking up the battery, it will be difficult to check items such as lights, speedometers, depthfinders, tachometers, bilge pumps, live-well pumps, and radios. Depending on the boat's age and condition, plan on replacing those items where any question exists. At worst you'll stay on the high side of your projected cost, and you may even be in for a pleasant surprise when you discover that they work.

As you look over the accessories, jot down any extras that may be included in the deal, such as docklines, anchors, rod holders, spare props,

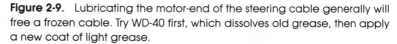

Figure 2-9. Lubricating the motor-end of the steering cable generally will free a frozen cable. Try WD-40 first, which dissolves old grease, then apply a new coat of light grease.

life jackets, etc. You'll need all these items anyway, so you should consider them when making an offer.

Summary

As I said earlier, the secret to surveying a used boat is education. Once you've decided on a design, research the builder and find out if they're still in operation. Prior to making an offer, try to list what parts will be needed, and get estimates from your local dealers and boatyards.

Crawl through boats until you've seen firsthand what effect the sun has on tarps, upholstery, and floor coverings. Probe floors and transoms with your awl until you can tell the difference between rotten and sound wood. Examine known leakers so you'll be able to spot similar symptoms when you come across them. You'll see no fiberglass flowerpots in the backyards of smart boat buyers.

THE "EXPERT'S" CHECKLIST

- ❏ Education is the key!
- ❏ Learn how boats are built.
- ❏ Know the difference between sound and rotten plywood.
- ❏ Avoid severely damaged boats.
- ❏ Check the gelcoat for crazing.
- ❏ Check the bottom of the hull for hairline cracks with rusty stains.
- ❏ Avoid metalflake finishes (unless you *really* think they look cool).
- ❏ Sight along the hull and look for checkered patterns.
- ❏ Determine the hull thickness at the transom and under the gunnels. Thin fiberglass here indicates weak construction.
- ❏ Check the keel for severe damage.
- ❏ Avoid most boats with cored hulls.
- ❏ Probe the floor for rot with your awl, especially along the boat's centerline and around the seats.
- ❏ Check the upholstery for cracks, rips, etc.

- ❏ Probe seat backs and bottoms for rot.
- ❏ Probe the transom for rot, especially around hardware.
- ❏ Sight along the top edge of the transom; is it straight?
- ❏ Probe *all* the plywood you can find.
- ❏ Operate shift, throttle, and steering cables.
- ❏ Try to operate all instruments and accessories.
- ❏ Check the wiring harness and connections.
- ❏ Make a list of all accessories and their condition.
- ❏ Have the motor (if there is one) checked by a mechanic.

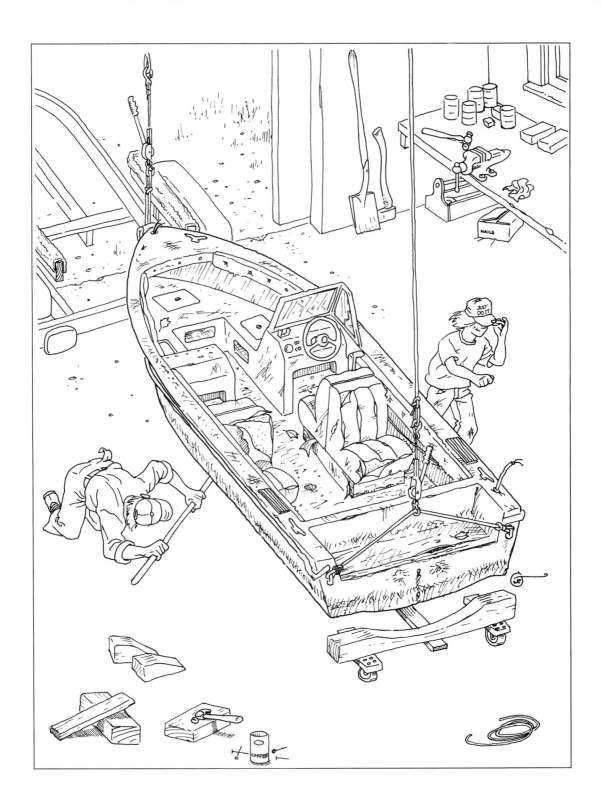

RUNABOUT RENOVATION

CHAPTER

3

Planning:
The Key to
a Successful Renovation

I don't know many boat nuts who at one time or another haven't said, ''I'd give my right arm for that boat.'' It's a figure of speech, of course, and we all know that no boat is worth an arm, or even a finger. Nevertheless, any boat restoration project involves using machinery that can easily cut wood or fiberglass. Think how easily that same machine can cut flesh and bone. If this project is to be fun, it must be safe.

Commonsense Safety

This book assumes that the reader is familiar with the operation of such common power tools as a circular saw, drill, and grinder. But even with abundant experience, certain phases of this project—removing the floor or replacing frames and stringers, for instance—will test your skills by putting you and those tools in awkward physical positions. Be certain of your footing and balance before turning on any power tools.

I have several pairs of jeans with neat little cuts just above the knees—near misses with a high-speed grinder. Let's face it: Despite dire warnings from the manufacturer, you'll probably have to remove the guards from the grinder to get into the corners and flush with the sides of the hull. Despite those same warnings, it's only natural to set down the grinder before the wheel comes to a complete stop. Ouch. The same applies to power saws. I assure you, guard or not, eventually they'll jump up and bite you if you aren't careful. Use common sense.

Use common sense about keeping a clean work area, too. It will have a positive, cumulative effect on safety and the overall quality of your work. It's particularly important to keep the inside of the boat as free of debris as possible. This is a prime place to slip and fall, usually with a whirring power tool in hand. I always keep a garbage can sitting next to the boat when removing a floor or transom and wing parts into it as they come out. I also keep a shop-vac handy inside the boat.

In short, a fair dose of patience and a bit of common sense will go a long way toward making the restoration project more enjoyable and safer.

Hazardous Materials

Although incautiously used power tools present the most obvious threat to your health and safety, a far more serious and less obvious threat is posed by fiberglass resin, paint, acetone, wood preservatives, and a variety of other materials you'll use.

The threat begins with the fiberglass dust created when grinding. Fiberglass is all but indestructible—and so's the dust. When inhaled into the lungs, it tends to stay. At a minimum, use good-quality, paper face filters when sanding. With age, polyester resin becomes brittle; when cut with a power saw, it chips and scatters. Wear a facemask and eye protection any time you're grinding, cutting, or sanding.

Even more insidious and a lot less noticeable are the fumes from paint, solvents, wood preservatives, and resin. Make sure your workspace is well ventilated, and invest in a dual-cartridge paint-spray respirator; wear it any time you're using a product that emits chemicals, such as the wood preservatives you'll use to treat your new plywood parts, or the acetone used to clean your tools and wipe down the boat before painting.

Many of today's marine paints contain a urethane base that emits chemicals such as aliphatic polyisocyanate, isocyanates, and many others I can't pronounce. These pose a constant health threat in any form, but are most dangerous when atomized through a paint sprayer. Once atomized, they will permeate the skin as well as enter the lungs. Most paints are more flammable when atomized, which means no open flames in your shop.

If you're planning to spray your boat, you'll need an oil-less air compressor and face piece to supply you with fresh air while spraying. Also invest in disposable coveralls and gloves (available from your local marine dealer or safety supply house). The coveralls should be made of a material impervious to chemicals (Tyvek, for instance). Also understand that the danger from these chemicals does not pass when you're through painting. Some two-part coating systems may take up to 72 hours to cure completely. During that curing process, the paints emit solvents and other chemicals into your work area. Be sure the area is well ventilated, either naturally or by using window fans, extractors, etc.

Don't throw dabs of solvents, paints, and resins down the drain; you may plug your drain, poison your groundwater, or eat a hole in your sewer pipes. Store leftovers in a metal container until you're finished, then dispose of the can according to your city or county regulations concerning toxic waste (call your fire department; they'll know what procedures you'll need to follow).

In short, there are some *very* dangerous chemicals used in today's marine paints. Read the cautions on every can and follow them to the letter. I certainly don't mean to frighten you away from an enjoyable and rewarding project, but I'd be remiss if I didn't stress the importance of safety when working with these products.

Safe work habits result as much from attitude as from a strict adherence to manufacturer's recommendations and cautions. Accept the fact that renovating your boat will take time. Approach every phase methodically and follow all the applicable safety rules. Aside from ensuring your safety, such an approach will help ensure a more professional finished product.

Tools and Equipment

You won't be far into your project before you realize that restoring an old boat is an imperfect science. My own repair methods and procedures grew out of necessity over time. In the early days of my business, I simply nodded my head "yes" when asked if I could fix something, *then* worried how I was going to do it. Over the years I was able to improve on my original methods, but it's entirely possible that, with imagination, you may be able to develop simpler approaches of your own, using tools other than those I list below. Be creative and flexible.

Aside from common hand tools such as a hammer, pry bars, a tape measure, chisels, etc., you'll need a substantial list of additional tools— although nothing exotic. I won't tell you to buy an automatic floor remover, if such a thing existed. Try to accumulate the tools you need before beginning the project. You may save yourself some aggravation later.

You'll need:

❏ A circular power saw. Because fiberglass dust is no better for tools than it is for lungs, I suggest using an older saw. Use a good carbide blade, though.

❏ Grinders. I use a 7-inch, 6,000-r.p.m. angle grinder on the floors and transoms, and a 4-inch grinder for roughing out the finish work on glass repairs.

Figure 3-1. You'll need a 1- by 6-inch fiberglass roller to work out air bubbles in the laminate and ensure all the glass fibers are saturated with resin.

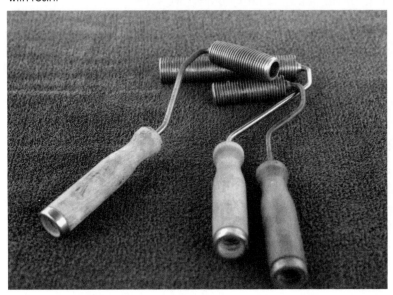

❑ A ³⁄₈-inch electric drill with a set of screwdriver bits. A good cordless drill is extremely handy.

❑ A saber saw. Among other tasks, you'll need one for seat repairs and cutting the floor pieces.

❑ Sanders. I prefer to use air-operated tools for sanding. Most projects require no more than a 5-inch, double-action sander, with a straight-line finishing sander for fairing glass repairs. If you don't have access to an air compressor, use a good electric, orbital finish sander and a 7-inch polisher-sander. Leave the belt sander in the tool cabinet; it can do too much damage too quickly to thin laminates.

❑ Fiberglassing tools. You'll need a 1- by 6-inch fiberglass roller. If there is no fiberglass supply house in your area, your local marine dealer may be able to order the rollers for you. If not, see Appendix B for some reputable mail-order distributors. You'll also need a variety of plastic spreaders, putty knives, paint rollers, and rubber or plastic gloves.

❑ A large rubber hammer.

❑ A pop-rivet gun. It'll be necessary only on specific designs. Check your boat for rivets before investing in one.

❑ Wood clamps and C-clamps.

❑ A shop-vac.

❑ An electric or hand stapler for replacing upholstery.

❑ At least two portable clamp-on lights.

❑ A caulking gun.

A Place To Work

I got into the boat repair business partly from necessity and partly by accident. I had been renting a fleet of 16 small sailboats on the beach of a local resort for a few years. Inevitably, the boats deteriorated into various states of disrepair. My humble operation had begun as a hobby, and it wasn't exactly a cash cow. When the boats reached the point where they needed repair, I had no choice but to locate a temporary facility and do the job myself.

Initially I arranged to rent a single stall in an auto dealership for a couple of months—just until I could complete the needed repairs on my own boats piled up in the parking lot. Within a couple of weeks, and without advertising, I had a constant flow of boat nuts stopping by to see what was going on. Soon they wanted to know if I could fix their boats, too. Before long I often had two boats jammed into the single stall and several fair-weather jobs sitting outside. Within two months I had made the switch from renting boats to repairing them.

That first summer I did the bulk of my repairs outside—which I recommend highly as a work area. Cleanup is easy, and there is simply no better ventilation available when sanding or working with resins and other chemicals (but remember what I said earlier about flushing toxic waste into yours or someone else's well; this stuff is nasty). Of course your progress will be subject to local weather conditions and curious neighbors, and when it comes time to paint you'll have to move the boat inside or build a temporary shelter over the work area, keeping in mind that proper ventilation is a *must*.

There are many other considerations. If your boat needs a new transom, you'll have to separate the hull and deck sections. As a rule, the deck sections of boats under 18 feet can be easily lifted from the hull and set aside with the help of a few friends. For most boats over 18 feet, you'll probably need some sort of hoist system, with sufficient ceiling height to allow it to function.

With the weight distributed, the average truss rafters found in a typical garage *probably* will take the weight of the deck section without shoring or additional supports. Depending on the size of the boat, the deck (less windshield) usually won't exceed 300 pounds. But again, this is an imperfect science, and unless you have access to the advice of a structural engineer, practice the age-old approach of "better safe than sorry." If you're doubtful about your rafters' strength, shore up beneath them.

If you're planning to replace the transom (and if the boat is under 18 feet), you'll find it easier to work on the boat if you lift it off the trailer and set it on two keel carts (more on these later). The boat will be lower and more accessible, and the absence of a trailer tongue will save a few nicked shins. If you're working in a garage with a concrete floor and a driveway, the carts will allow you to move the boat easily from one to the other.

You'll have to hang come-a-longs, a block and tackle, or a chain hoist from the existing rafters to lift the boat off the trailer. Few boats in the 16- to 18-foot range will exceed 800 to 1,200 pounds with the outboard and deck hardware removed, but that's still a lot of weight. To be safe, shore up the load-bearing rafters of a typical garage by placing adequate timbers across several rafters to distribute the boat's weight; support the ends with 4 × 4s. You want to hoist your boat off the trailer, not pull your garage down on top of your boat.

When painting, I usually flip boats 18 feet and under completely upside down and set them on carts. It simply makes the process of sanding, fairing, and painting much easier. Alone, and armed with nothing but a little ingenuity and a few hoists and carts, flipping a boat is not an impossible task, but give it some thought: At best, it will leave you with a severe case of the jitters. You'll also need a 20-foot-wide space, minimum, and fairly high ceilings.

When contemplating your work area, keep in mind that the clouds of dust produced by sanding fiberglass will settle in and on everything. To a degree (and sometimes at the expense of ventilation) it can be controlled by hanging plastic or tarps around the work area, but the stuff seems to seek out every crack. If your available space will allow it, keep a hose handy to wash down the floor and walls after sweeping.

A final consideration is proper lighting. There simply is no better light than that provided by mother nature. The more windows in your workspace, the better. But even with ample natural and overhead light, there are at least two instances when you'll need portable, clamp-on lights and convenient outlets.

The first will occur when you start sanding and discover some additional areas of crazed gelcoat that you missed during your survey. These are extremely hard to see without proper light, and even harder to see when filled with sanding dust. Locating minute cracks in the gelcoat will require close inspection with a good portable light.

Second, when it comes time to paint you'll need lights that can be moved around the boat and adjusted to different angles. Without proper lighting it's nearly impossible to ensure that the paint is applied evenly.

In summary, there are no hard-and-fast rules for choosing a work area. The fact is, you'll have to make do with whatever is available. However, the space should be well lighted, well ventilated, and, if possible, isolated. And do try to give yourself at least 6 feet of workspace all the way around the boat.

Hoisting the Boat from the Trailer

If your boat doesn't need extensive hull repairs or painting, you don't really need to remove it from the trailer. You can replace floors and most other repairs with the boat sitting on a stabilized trailer. It will be far easier to work on, however, if it's sitting on carts, or even a few old tires. Lifting the boat from the trailer is not a major project.

We've already discussed distributing the boat's weight and shoring up rafters when lifting it, but there are a couple of other tips that may be of use. In boats of 20 feet and longer, the builder may have included lifting points designed to accommodate the weight of the boat; if they appear sound, there's no reason not to use them. Usually they'll be located on the boat's centerline, fore and aft. They may be concealed under hatches in the floor or, in some cases, lifting rings may be mounted on a reinforced area of the deck.

Such lifting points are uncommon in the typical 15- to 17-foot runabout. I've used the bow eye and the stern towing eyes consistently without a problem, but don't take their soundness for granted; check them carefully before attempting to lift the boat. If they're bent, rusted, or pulled away from the hull, replace them. You'll want new ones anyway.

Pay particular attention to the backing plate behind the bow eye. Often this was just a piece of 1/2-inch plywood sealed with a bit of chopped fiberglass. If it's rotten or weak, build a new one and install it before lifting the boat.

Don't attach the metal hooks of a hoist or come-a-long directly to the eyes. When they begin to take a strain they'll angle into the hull, leaving you with, at best, scarred gelcoat. To save an unnecessary repair, tie a loop of 3/4-inch nylon line through the bow eye, long enough to extend above the deck at least a foot. Attach the lifting hooks to the loop. Under strain, the loop will be free to tighten on each side of the bow. Place a piece of heavy carpet or plywood between the line and the aluminum extrusion that covers the hull/deck joint to prevent any damage.

At the stern, tie a 3/4-inch line between the two stern towing eyes.

Again, make it long enough for the loop to extend about a foot above the transom. Under strain, you'll be able to center the lifting hook as the boat settles on the lifting points.

Lift the boat evenly until it just clears the trailer, no more than a few inches. Now swing the boat around some. This little exercise will relieve you of a minor case of the jitters and test your rafters, hoisting system, and knots. If the boat should drop, it can only land on the trailer. Once you're satisfied that your system is sound and secure, move the trailer out of the way and replace it with your carts or cradle (for building instructions, read on).

A word about knots is in order. When lifting boats, I use nothing but a bowline. Even using nylon line, which occasionally tends to slip and always stretches, I've never seen a bowline come loose. In addition, the knot can sit for months under strain and still be undone with your bare hands. I don't care for knots that can only be undone with a sharp knife. If you're not familiar with the bowline, study Figure 3-2. You'll find it has many uses around your boat.

Keel Carts

Although they're available, I never found it necessary to invest in commercial carts to move boats of this size. My favorite carts consist of nothing more than four 2 × 6s, bolted together at the corners, with a set of heavy-duty casters (check hardware stores; the bigger the wheel, the easier it rolls) underneath and the contact points covered with foam and carpet. The carts can be customized to the shape of your hull by nailing on blocks of 2 × 4s until the boat sits level and solid.

The size of the cart will naturally depend on the size of the boat, but I wouldn't go much over 2 by 4 feet with 2 × 6s. If your boat requires larger carts for adequate stability, move up to 4 × 4s.

If you'll be moving the boat in and out of your garage, nail a 1 × 4 between the two carts to keep them from separating when you're moving the boat around. Occasionally, one cart will move and the other won't.

Cradles

To do bottom repairs, big boatyards routinely put 40-footers on blocks or stands. In my opinion it's a much safer practice on boats of that size than on the smaller ones we're interested in. The heavier the boat and, therefore, the greater the downward force, the safer the practice becomes. A

Figure 3-2. Tying a bowline.

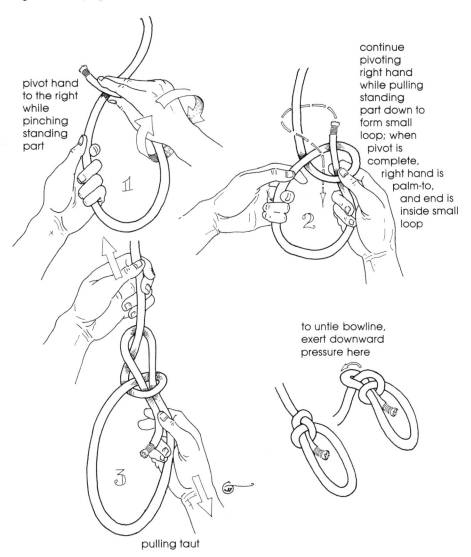

pivot hand to the right while pinching standing part

1

continue pivoting right hand while pulling standing part down to form small loop; when pivot is complete, right hand is palm-to, and end is inside small loop

2

to untie bowline, exert downward pressure here

3

pulling taut

large boat is less susceptible to lateral pressure from wind, accidental bumps, and a group of kibitzing friends leaning on it.

Because I have difficulty suppressing visions of being squashed like an ant, I've never been entirely comfortable working on a boat sitting on blocks. Personally, I take no chances. I build a cradle.

The cradle described here takes very little time to build; I've used it

Figure 3-3. Moving your boat on keel carts will make renovating easy. Don't waste your money on commercial carts—these homemade specimens are easy to build.

(Figure 3-3 continued.)

many, many times on boats of this size, and I trust it to be safe and secure. This isn't the only way to build a cradle, and you may select an entirely different design, but keep in mind that your objective is two-fold: First, the cradle must be solid and well built. Second, it should not interfere with your work under the boat more than absolutely necessary. Any areas covered by the cradle will have to be sanded and painted separately. With the following design, those areas can be touched up once the boat is back on the trailer.

Take a look at the boat's stern, where the sides and the bottom of the hull meet. Many designs provide convenient flat spots at these corners that serve nicely as points on which to rest the boat. This generally is one of the strongest areas of the hull, and the cradle won't hinder your work to a great extent. If your boat doesn't have a convenient flat spot on the bottom, you'll have to cut a block for each side of the cradle to conform to the hull shape.

The cradle should be constructed much like the stud walls of a house, using 2 × 6s. Measure across the hull from corner to corner, and cut two pieces of 2 × 6 the same length to serve as top and bottom plates.

Next, determine the height of the cradle. If you'll be lying under the boat sanding the hull, estimate a height to give you a comfortable, average reach with the tools you'll use. That becomes the height of your cradle. Cut enough 2 × 6s so that they can be nailed on 16-inch centers the length of the plates. This will be the back wall.

Build two side walls and nail them to the back wall. These usually needn't be more than 2 or 3 feet long, but that will depend on the length of your boat. The forward vertical 2 × 6s should be doubled, and they must extend forward far enough so that there is no danger of the entire cradle kicking out backward.

Nail a 2 × 4 across the bottom of the side walls to prevent them from spreading. Depending on the height of the cradle, the shape of your hull, and your inclination toward safety, you may also want to nail a brace from the bottom 2 × 4 to the top ends of the side walls.

Hoist the boat until you have enough room to slide the cradle under the stern. Lower the boat onto the cradle, making sure that the boat is level and the cradle is taking the full weight of the stern. Use the bow hoist to raise the bow a few inches so you can slide a stack of blocks under the keel; the fewer blocks you use, the more stable they'll be. To find a level spot on the keel, you may have to place the blocks right in the middle of the boat, depending on your hull design. Lower the bow onto the blocks and gently test your work. Keep in mind that because the boat is resting on only three points, it will still be susceptible to a lateral jolt at the bow. As an added precaution, leave the hoisting lines in place with enough strain on them to hold the boat if the cradle or blocks give out.

On paper these projects may sound complicated, time consuming, and expensive. In some cases it is simply necessary, and in others it becomes a matter of convenience. If you've opted to build carts and you buy new casters, you may invest $40 to $50, but it should take no more than a couple of hours to put them together. You should be able to nail the cradle together in less than an hour, and it isn't even necessary to buy new lumber. Before the project is over I think you'll find that either project was worth the investment in time and money.

A PROPER WORK AREA

❏ A lot of this stuff is *poison*. Work outside whenever possible.

❏ Other than minor repairs are best done off the trailer. Do you have enough ceiling height to hang a hoist?

❏ Shore up rafters or collar beams before hoisting your boat.

❏ If you're flipping the boat over, you'll need 20 feet of uncluttered space.

❏ A floor drain is extremely handy, but *don't* dump toxic chemicals down it.

❏ The more light, the better.

❏ The more ventilation, the better.

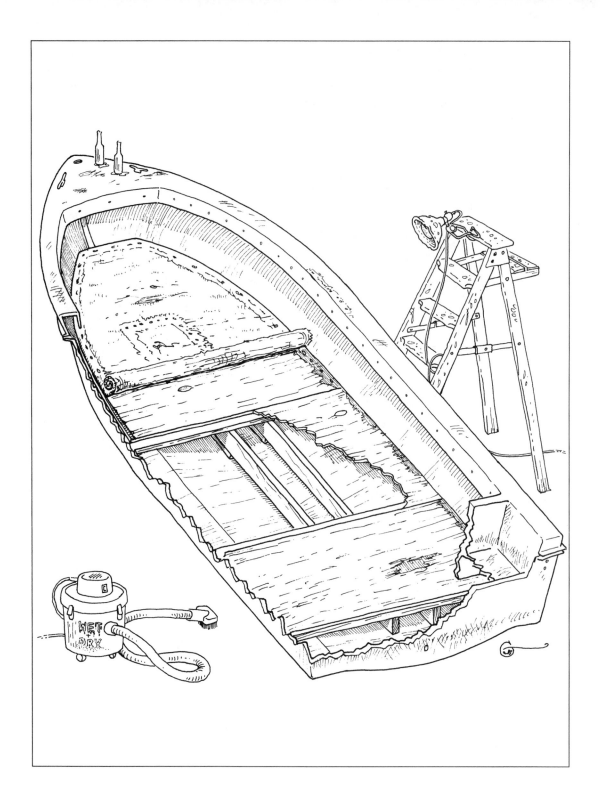

CHAPTER

4

Out with the Old Floor, In with the New

In the Preface I hinted that parts of the renovation process would be little more than hard, dirty work. Removing a rotten floor is what I had in mind. By the time you've got the rotten floor out, you may be ready to chuck the entire project and buy a new boat. Don't do it! Once the floor is out, the hard part is done. The rest is just plain fun. Besides, properly installed, your new floor will be far superior to the original—satisfying knowledge for the true boat lover.

As with each phase of the renovation, satisfactory results depend on forethought and preparation.

Unique Designs

Although I've mentioned it before, this might be a good time to mention it again: For the purposes of illustration, this book is based on renovating a "typical" 16-foot runabout, with a V-hull and a covered bow, from the 1960s to early 1970s. Bassboats, tri-hulls, and open-bow boats all present distinct problems unique to each design, but the actual procedure for removing and replacing a floor is much the same for all fiberglass boats of any vintage—naturally with a few exceptions.

As we saw in Chapter 1, all boats of this era were constructed in two sections, the deck and the hull. The hull contains a plywood floor, glassed in place over stringers and frames. Figure 4-1 shows the open hull section, with the floor glassed in place, of a new Larson. Figure 4-2 shows the for-

Figure 4-1. The plywood floor, glassed in place over stringers and frames. This construction is typical for most runabouts built in the 1960s and 1970s, and many of them today as well.

Figure 4-2. The forward deck unit of a bowrider, with console and forward sitting area molded in place.

ward part of a deck section, with the seats and other accessories in place, ready to be attached to the hull. (These aren't from the same boat, but for the purpose of explanation it doesn't matter.) The older Larsons and Foresters used this design, and I'm sure there are many others.

As you can see, the boat has an open bow. Part of the molded deck section forward of the instrument panel hangs down to form the forward floor pan. When this is set into the hull section, it will rest on the forward end of the plywood floor glassed into the hull. In my experience, this forward piece of plywood seldom rots to the extent of the rest of the floor. However, because the edges of the plywood meet where the molded deck ends, it can happen. If it has in fact rotted and must be replaced, you'll have to separate the hull and deck sections to do it. And this warrants a caution.

With the hull and deck sections separated *and* the floor removed, there is little left to support the hull's shape. Hull rigidity depends on the floor *and* the hull/deck joint. If you remove the deck section from the hull, then measure, cut, and install a new floor, the floor pieces likely will be too wide, which will spread the hull further. When you try to reinstall the deck section, it won't fit—a bit like trying to put an undersize lid on a Tupperware bowl.

The same problem may occur if you have a boat that needs both a new floor and a new transom. Resist the temptation to replace them at the same time—another lesson I had to learn the hard way. Do the floor first, with the exception of the piece that meets the transom. Once the floor is in, *then* separate the hull and deck and replace the transom. After the new transom is in, finish the last piece of floor.

There's another unique design that requires a slightly different approach than the generic one described in this chapter. Lund, Forester, and I'm sure others, built some boats in the 16-foot range in the mid-1970s that were considered early bassboats. The floors were flat and the interiors open, and they usually had a couple of pedestal seats and perhaps a live well, but they were very narrow.

And this narrow beam is what sets them apart from the boat we discuss in this chapter. They were designed so that the floor could be built from standard, uncut, 4 × 8 plywood sheets laid longitudinally from stern to bow. This resulted in great economy, I'm sure, but it also resulted in a cramped boat that tended to roll a bit much for my taste.

The floors can be difficult to replace, too. The deck section often had molded fiberglass live wells, seats, or rod boxes set on top of the floor. Because of the narrow beam, there is no way to replace the floor without separating the hull and deck. As we've seen, that opens the possibility that the hull will spread out of shape.

Don't despair; it can be done. We know that the floor pieces are 4 feet wide. When you have the boat ready for its new floor, lay the plywood in place and check to see how snugly the edges fit, then clamp a single piece of 1 × 4 along both sides of the hull to keep them rigid. Tie three or four ropes around the hull the length of the boat and tighten them gently until the hull pulls together and the new plywood fits snugly in the floor/hull joint. (Try to do most of your work from the outside to keep your weight out of the boat.) Keep an eye on that hull/floor joint while you're working. If it spreads a little, tighten the ropes a bit.

Again, this is a unique design that didn't survive too many years. If you own one, this process will make more sense to you after reading the rest of this chapter.

Materials

Before you begin replacing the old floor, you've got some runnin' around to do. For a job like this, you'll want all the materials handy. In some areas, specialized items such as resin, fiberglass, and flotation foam are hard to find and expensive. With a little looking, though, they can be found (see Appendix B for some ideas). The rest of the floor is made from plywood and lumber, available at any good lumberyard.

Floors for boats of this era inevitably were made of plywood, usually 1/2 inch thick for our typical 16-foot boat. The boat nut embarking on his first renovation may be inclined to replace his floor with marine plywood. I don't recommend it. For this application, marine plywood simply isn't necessary; the cost of four sheets may well exceed the cost of the boat. Builders don't use it for the same reason.

Pressure-treated ply will work, but it's often made from yellow pine, which is very hard and difficult to work with. The pressure-treating process makes it even harder and seems to affect glue adhesion, too: I've seen the edges delaminate in some applications, and it doesn't accept resin as well as other plywoods.

Its low cost may tempt you to use particle, or chip, board, but it's no-where near as strong as laminated plywood. And even though it's manu-factured with exterior adhesives, it doesn't stand up under constant moisture—the inevitable condition existing in the bilge of all boats. I'd avoid it.

Construction-grade plywood (CDX) will suffice, but it usually has in-terior voids in the laminate, which can lead to weak spots in the floor as well as provide ideal spots for rot to take hold.

My choice is AC plywood. Originally, it was designed for interior ap-plications where moisture was not expected to be a problem. The expert at my local lumberyard assures me that this is no longer the case, and that all plywoods today are glued with exterior glue. Nonetheless, when asking for AC plywood, it can't hurt to specify exterior grade.

AC plywood is sanded on one side, which provides a nice surface with which to work. Because it provides a good blend of affordability, strength, and durability, it's my choice for a job like this. Any neighborhood lumberyard should be able to supply it.

In addition to finding a source for plywood, you'll also have to find one for polyester resin and fiberglass mat. Resin can be found in nearly every autoparts or marine store, but usually only at full retail price—as much as $35 a gallon over the counter. You'll need 5 gallons of polyester laminating resin and its accompanying catalyst (included) for the floor and substructure of most 16-footers, which means you're looking at $175 over the counter.

To cut costs, get on the phone and call around until you find someone who'll sell you resin and catalyst in bulk. If there's a boat shop in your area, start there. Also check with autobody shops specializing in Corvette repairs. Some of you may be lucky enough to have a business in your area that specializes in fiberglass fabrication. Any of these businesses are likely to have polyester resin in 55-gallon drums, and may well be willing to part with enough for your project.

When I was in business I paid approximately $8 a gallon for resin bought by the drum. If a do-it-yourselfer came into my shop with his own containers for resin and catalyst, I sold it to him for $16 a gallon. He saved at least 50 percent, and I still made a handsome profit.

Given the markup on resin purchased in small quantities, it will be well worth your effort to shop around. The same shops should also carry fiberglass mat and cloth in bulk rolls, and similar savings can be had.

If you're in the back of beyond and can't find a fiberglass supplier, mail order (see Appendix B) is an option, but the freight on heavy jugs of resin and oversize bolts of cloth will quickly eat up any savings. In this case it may behoove you to pack up and head for the big city (after letting your fingers do the walking); the savings will probably pay for the trip.

Removing the Old Floor

Begin by stripping the boat's interior of all the equipment attached to the floor, or any accessories that may get in the way of removing the floor pieces.

Start with the seats and seat bases. The bases normally will be attached to the floor with Phillips-head, stainless steel screws. With the proper bit chucked in a reversible electric drill, these screws should back out with little resistance. If one should prove stubborn, slide a pry bar under the seat base and apply upward pressure; it should back right out or, if the floor is rotten, pull out.

Move aft toward the transom. Boats of this size generally have a storage area under the splash well for the battery, portable fuel tanks, and the like. Some builders enclosed this area with sliding doors; some used a piece of upholstery snapped to a strip of wood screwed to the floor. There may also be an upholstered piece of plywood at the top of the splash well, usually attached with machine screws or studs. Whatever's there, you'll have to remove it.

Like the seat bases, structural components and other equipment, such as battery and fuel tank tie-downs, will be attached to the floor with stainless steel sheetmetal screws. Remove all this stuff and set it aside. If there is a bilge pump, cut the wires several inches from the pump and remove it. Be sure to leave the wires long enough so that they can be spliced later.

There may be panels on the side of the hull that serve as catch-alls for fishing rods and general boat stuff. These usually are constructed of $1/4$- or $3/8$-inch plywood covered with matching upholstery and are attached

Figure 4-3. When taking up the old floor, you'll have to remove the side panels, plus whatever covers the storage area under the splash well.

with sheetmetal screws to a piece of ¾-inch wood glassed to the hull. The panels will have to come off, but the piece glassed to the hull can stay unless it's rotten, too.

On designs with an open bow, there may be bulkheads, generally covered with upholstery or the same material that covers the floor, that support the deck directly under the windshield. In many cases these too must be removed.

Once you've stripped everything from the boat's interior, you're ready to start demolishing the old floor. The first step is to strip away and trash any vinyl or carpet covering. Even though it may appear to be in good shape, much of the backing will stick to the floor when you pull it up. There is no point in trying to reuse it.

Once you get the floor covering off, the floor's true condition will be obvious. Most builders sprayed the wood floor with chopped fiberglass and resin. This was meant to shed water and, presumably, prevent rot. It usually did shed water for a few years, but unfortunately, it did little to prevent rot. In many cases, the ever-present moisture in the bilge caused the floor to rot from the bottom up (we'll slather on plenty of wood preservative to prevent this happening). With a pry bar and your hands (wear gloves), pull up as much of the chopped glass as possible, and vacuum out the boat. Now you can study the original construction.

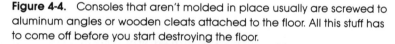

Figure 4-4. Consoles that aren't molded in place usually are screwed to aluminum angles or wooden cleats attached to the floor. All this stuff has to come off before you start destroying the floor.

With the one exception I mentioned earlier, most boats of this length are about 60 inches wide at the widest point. Because the floor pieces are cut from 4 × 8 plywood, they're all 48 inches wide, cut to length to conform to the width and shape of the hull.

Note where the floor joints are on your boat. Locate all edges that are still intact and visible. Take as many measurements of the floor pieces as you can, and draw a sketch of the floor. Depending on the degree of rot, you may be able to get accurate measurements of each of the floor pieces, which may save you a step.

Also, check the hull/floor joint where plywood meets fiberglass. Take note of the extra glass that was added as reinforcement to this area. Try to learn as much as you can about the floor's original construction; this will make the subsequent reconstruction go much easier. If the floor is totally gone, don't panic. We'll deal with that situation later in this chapter.

When you have an accurate, measured sketch of the floor drawn, with as many construction details added as you can find, set your drawing in a safe place, get out your grinder (with a 40-grit disk), and put on your coveralls and dust mask. It's time to get dirty.

If this is the first time you've used a high-torque grinder, take it easy. Like children, sometimes they bite and kick. Grip it firmly and set it down on the floor a few times until you get a feel for it. Try it on a waste piece of wood to see what kind of damage it can do. In the last chapter I mentioned what kind of damage it can do to blue jeans.

At the hull/floor joint, grind away the fiberglass until the edge of the plywood is visible. There will be a distinct line where the edge of the wood meets the hull. If you couldn't get accurate measurements before,

Figure 4-5. The floor pieces are cut from standard 4 X 8, ½-inch plywood.

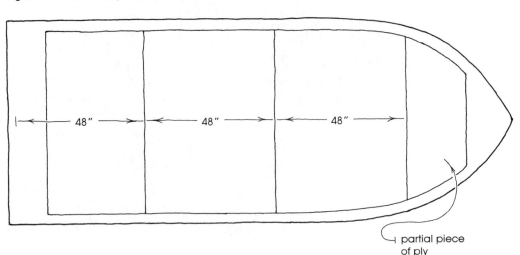

partial piece of ply

you should be able to do so now.

Next, set your circular saw to cut about ⅝ inch deep. This will cut through the ½-inch plywood floor and the chopped glass covering typical of most 16-foot boats. Don't set your saw too deep for the first cut; you don't want to cut too deeply into the stringers and frames below. Also, when working near the floor/hull joint of some boats it is very easy to cut a nice clean slice right through the bottom—another lesson I learned the hard way.

Cut the entire floor into garbage-can size pieces that can be pried from the stringers and frames. This will take a bit of doing. There simply is no easy way to go at this grueling process of cutting, hacking, and making small pieces out of big ones until the old floor is in the garbage.

Once the floor is out you'll have to clean up the floor/hull joint with an old chisel and/or your grinder. Try to preserve the original joint line and form as much as possible. You'll save yourself some work later.

Clean the inside of the boat and vacuum the bilge well so you can study the substructure.

Flotation, Frames, and Stringers

When you've got the old floor out, the bilge, frames, stringers, and flotation will be exposed. Most builders used one of two types of flotation in boats of this vintage: blocks of Styrofoam flopped haphazardly into the bilge, or expanded foam.

Figure 4-6. After removing the carpet, cut the old plywood floor pieces along the dotted lines with a circular saw to make them more manageable.

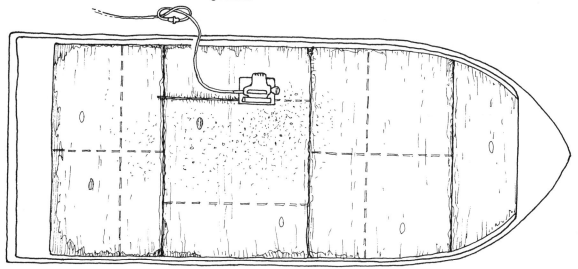

Careful builders installed the floor, drilled holes through it, and forced in expandable foam, which filled every nook and cranny in the bilge, with the exception of the bilge channel. This method certainly had more inherent longevity than loose Styrofoam blocks, but prior to the advent of closed-cell foam, it too became waterlogged if the floor leaked over time, and most did. Dig a hole in the foam—whichever kind you have—with your bare hands. You'll soon know if it's wet. If it is, dig it out and throw it away. You could try to dry it for years without success.

Once you've dug out all the foam, inspect the stringers and frames carefully for rot. (Semantics aside, I'll call all longitudinal supports *stringers*, and lateral supports *frames*.) If they're bad, take the measurements for your sketch and remove them, paying close attention to how they were constructed and attached originally. Be sure to take down enough measurements and make a good enough sketch so you can put things back together the way they were built. You may even be able to remove the originals intact to use as patterns.

It is more common to find rotten frames than stringers, and fortu-

Figure 4-7. The layout of stringers and frames will depend on the builder, but this is typical.

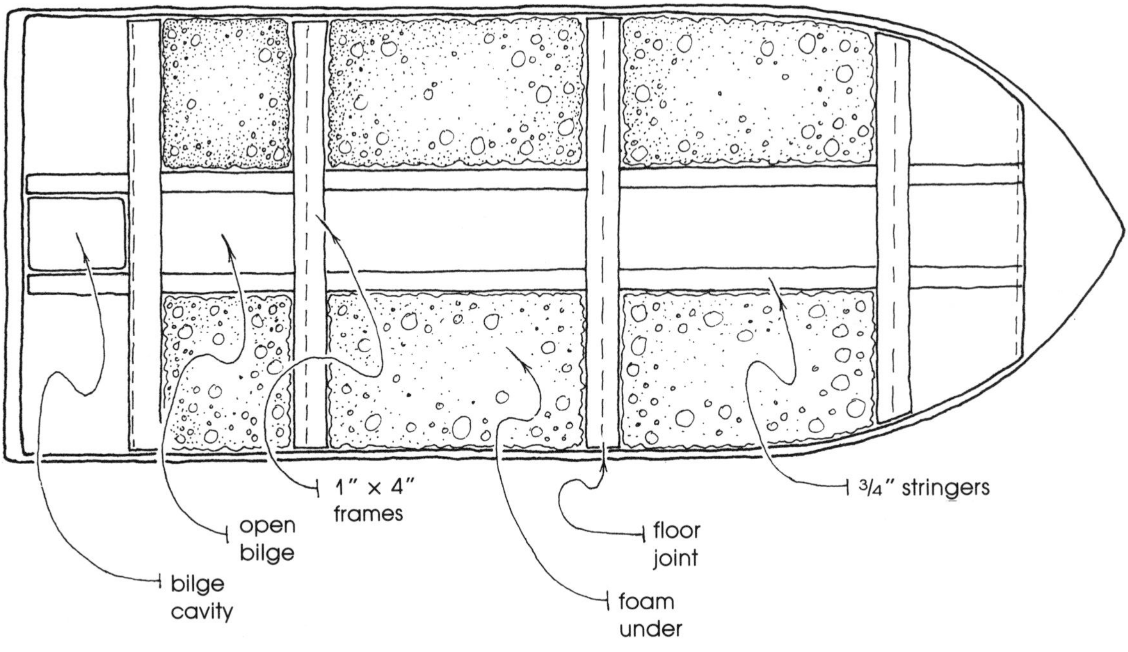

bilge cavity

open bilge

1" × 4" frames

foam under

floor joint

¾" stringers

nately they are easier to replace. The stringers may be a bit more difficult, but only because they're longer. In either case, simply pay attention to the original dimensions of the material and methods of construction. If I seem to be repeating that over and over, think about the time you took the alarm clock apart to see how it worked. Of course you didn't make sketches along the way, did you? And you couldn't get it back together again, either. Right?

Often, stringers and frames were covered with a piece of fiberglass mat, which served to bond the boat's substructure (stringers and frames) with the floor. In most cases you'll have to grind off the mat to get at the bad stringers and frames.

The builder probably attached the frames and stringers with staples or galvanized nails. This is another place where we part company. Use only stainless steel sheetmetal screws. They'll last as long as you own the boat, and although they're roughly three times more expensive than galvanized screws, this will add no more than $10 to the cost of the restoration—well worth it.

The builders and I part company over what material to use for the substructure, too. I've seen cedar stringers and pine frames; I've seen what looked like rough-sawn pallet lumber; I've seen wood that I simply couldn't identify. In short, some builders seem to use almost anything they have lying around. Since you're putting in all this work renovating the boat, I assume you'd like it to last a while.

Cedar and redwood are naturally resistant to rot, and I've used them in a few instances. But because they're softwoods, they don't hold screws well over time unless the pieces are also glassed together. Treated oak holds screws well and lasts forever, and it would be my choice if it weren't so expensive.

We are fortunate today that most lumberyards carry a good stock of pressure-treated fir or yellow pine (depending on where you live) in the most common dimensions. I highly recommend it for new frames and stringers. Pressure-treated wood is rot-free for decades, even submerged, and both fir and yellow pine are strong, hold screws well, and accept resin well enough for this application.

If you're on a strict budget, however, remember that the builders proved that nearly anything will work—at least for a while. But keep in mind that untreated wood won't last. Standard lumberyard-dimension stock will need at least two coats of a good wood preservative, which must be thoroughly dry before you attempt to apply resin.

Some builders didn't even use stringers and frames; others used frames but not stringers. In any event, if you've paid attention and taken accurate measurements of those pieces that need replacing, the process is pretty straightforward. Stringers normally will be notched to accept 1 × 4 frames on 4-foot centers. Just screw your new ones in place.

On the rare occasion when it's necessary to replace both stringers and frames, cut out all of the pieces according to your sketch and set them in place. Attach them with screws and check to make sure that the frames are flush with the bottom of the hull/floor joint. If you find a couple of high spots, grind off the bottom of the stringers where necessary. Custom fit everything. Once you're satisfied that the assembly is flat and true, glass the stringers in place (see below) using a strip of mat run down their entire length.

I know this sounds a bit complicated, but with your boat opened up you'll see how very simple it really is. A typical 16-footer will have only two stringers and three or four frames, depending on design. The stringers will probably be notched for the frames, making their replacement a simple project.

Installing New Flotation

Once you've replaced any rotten stringers and frames, it's time to tackle the flotation. Theoretically, all boats of this size should have enough flotation to stay afloat when filled with water. There is a formula for determining this (1 cubic foot of foam will support roughly 50 pounds), but we needn't concern ourselves with math. Just follow this simple rule: With the exception of the bilge channel, which runs from the bow to the drain plug in the stern, fill every crack and crevice below floor level with foam. That may sound like an ambitious project, but it's actually quite simple, although a bit expensive.

Companies such as Evercoat and Boat Armor produce foams for marine applications, either in aerosol cans, which require no mixing, or in a two-part package mixed one-to-one (a 2-gallon kit, enough for most runabouts, sells for around $75). Both expand rapidly to fill voids and are fast drying. I prefer to use the two-part mix, which is generally half the cost of aerosol foam and expands more quickly, too. Unlike Styrofoam and the open-cell foams used in many older boats, the new urethane foams will not readily absorb water or disintegrate when they come in contact with polyester resin.

As with most of these products, *read the safety precautions on the can*. Foam adheres to practically everything and is difficult to remove. Cut the top from a 1-gallon plastic milk jug (save the handle) and pour the two parts into the jug, mixing according to the directions; they'll begin to react almost immediately. Pour the foam into the desired void, where it will expand and harden in a matter of minutes. If you're not quick, you'll find yourself with a miniature volcano erupting in your hand, so have the area to be filled ready and mix the stuff right in the boat.

You'll probably misjudge the quantity needed on your first try, and you'll watch, mildly panicked, as the foam expands well above the level of the stringers and frames. Relax. Once it hardens, cut away the excess with a standard handsaw, whose flexible blade will allow you to trim the foam to fit. Save those pieces and stuff them into corners and cracks.

Once you've foamed the voids, it's important to seal any area where the new foam may be exposed to water. Although the new foams won't soak up water like Styrofoam, if left exposed long enough they will eventually take on water.

How To Work with Fiberglass and Resin

From this point on, you'll be mixing resin and fillers and laying fiberglass mat and cloth. If you don't spend the time to learn the proper technique and accept the fact that there are certain rules that *must* be followed, you'll waste your time and money. Let's take a few minutes to discuss how to do things right.

A gallon of polyester resin generally comes with a 1-ounce plastic tube of catalyst, normally enough to cure the entire gallon. As you can see, we're talking *drops* of catalyst. The amount used (more catalyst equals faster curing) will depend on how quickly you want the resin to cure, the prevailing humidity and temperature (an extremely humid or very cool day will retard the curing process, while a hot, dry day will speed it up), and the specific application. The formula that works one day may not be quite right the next; there simply are no hard-and-fast rules for mixing formulas.

Generally speaking, a normal coat of polyester resin will cure in two to four hours. When you're laying the mat on your new floor, four is preferable to two. The extended curing time will allow the resin to saturate the plywood and ensure proper adhesion. If you mix it too "hot" (too much catalyst) you'll end up with a sheet of cured mat *lying on top* of your new floor.

On the other hand, if you're repairing a small gouge in the hull you can mix the resin with extra catalyst and throw a heat lamp on the repair. It'll probably cure in 30 minutes.

After many years and as many snafus, I got to the point where I could pour the resin in a coffee can or milk jug, pour in the catalyst right from the bottle, and somehow come up with the right formula. Since you're probably working on your first, and maybe only, project, you won't have that luxury.

You can, however, experiment, and I recommend—no, I insist—that you do so. Get four paper cups and fill them with 4 ounces of resin. Add one drop of catalyst to one, two to another, three to the next, and four to the last. Mix each one *thoroughly* (though don't use the same mixing stick; it'll just move varying amounts of catalyst from container to container) and spread a thin coat on a piece of plywood, jotting down the time of application for each mixture. Check them periodically until they cure rock-hard. When each cures, jot down the time, and you'll have a fair idea of cure time and how much catalyst you'll need to use in a given situation.

No doubt you'll notice that your cup with four drops of catalyst is extremely hot—literally; you'll actually feel the heat when you check it. You'll probably never find a use for resin mixed this hot, but it's a useful example that may save you a few bucks later.

It goes without saying that you should read the mixing instructions on the can. Many will be as vague as I have been, but that is the nature of the beast. Specificity and polyester resin just don't appear in the same sentence. And when they say mix it thoroughly, they mean it. If you apply a poorly mixed formula to an area the size of your boat floor, you'll end up with wet spots that simply won't cure.

The second point that I want to make here is the importance of proper preparation. *Resin will not adhere to wet or dirty fiberglass*. Every area to be glassed must be clean and dry.

In every instance where fiberglass joins fiberglass, old or new, cleaning means roughing the surface with your grinder (or sander with 40-grit paper), making sure to extend the cleaning beyond the intended area to be glassed by a few inches, then wiping down the area thoroughly with acetone.

Acetone is nasty stuff, but it's cheap, can be found in nearly any hardware or marine store, and is the only product I know of that will dissolve polyester resin, but only when it's wet. It evaporates quickly, so I usually keep two coffee cans, about half full, sealed with the plastic lids. Immediately after using a roller or any other tool, I wash them in the first can and let them soak in the second. This is the only way you'll keep your tools clean. If you should slop a little resin down the side of your boat, stop what you're doing and wipe it down with acetone. It won't damage the gelcoat.

I'll throw in a few reminders as we go through the various projects, but try to remember these fundamental rules. They are important.

You'll also want to remember (you'd better remember) these safety tips:

❑ Polyester resin is about 40 percent styrene—a strong skin and mucous membrane irritant. Always wear a respirator when working with polyester resin.

❑ Catalyst can splash when poured. Wear eye protection.

❑ Acetone causes severe dermatitis, and in large quantities can damage your nervous system. As if that weren't enough, its vapors are explosive (and polyester-resin vapors are flammable). *Don't smoke, don't tolerate open flames, and don't use electric tools (they spark) around the stuff.*

❑ *Always* wear gloves and a respirator, and keep your workspace well ventilated.

Installing the New Floor

Now, with new stringers and frames in place and leveled and the voids filled with foam, you're ready to cut the individual pieces of plywood for the floor. As we've seen, in most cases you can take measurements from the old floor and make an accurate sketch of the pieces you'll need to cut. But if you bought a boat that's been sitting out in the grove for five years, the floor may have turned to dust when you started to tear into it. Not to worry.

Find several large pieces of cardboard to use as templates (try your local furniture or mattress store), and cut them into 4-foot widths to represent plywood. Begin at the stern and measure from one side of the *hull* to the other at the transom. Move 4 feet forward, where there will be some sort of lateral frame, and take your second measurement. Cut your cardboard long on both ends so that you can set it in place, and trim it along the hull/floor joints to conform with the original. Take care not to cut your template too short; you don't want to have to fill in a large mistake.

Once you're satisfied with the fit of the first piece of cardboard, leave it in place and continue the process forward until you've built a cardboard floor. Transfer your templates to your plywood and cut the actual floor pieces to shape with a saber saw. In some cases the edges of the forward pieces of plywood may need to be beveled slightly to fit snugly against the hull. This is easy: Just tilt the bed of your saber saw to the approximate angle of the hull.

Once you've cut all of the plywood floor pieces, put them in the boat and make sure they fit properly. If they need custom fitting, take off the high spots with your small grinder and a coarse grinding disk.

NOTE: If your boat also needs a new transom, the *first* piece of flooring that joins the transom will have to be cut down from 48 inches to 24 inches wide. Set aside the 2-foot piece that would have joined the transom until after you've installed the new one. This will give you room to remove the transom when the time comes.

Once you have all the pieces nicely fitted, it's time to treat your floor pieces with two coats of a good wood preservative. Be sure to allow the recommended drying time between coats and follow all safety rules of the product. Most preservatives contain toxic materials that should not be inhaled or allowed to come in contact with the skin. This is a good time to wear your facemask and surgical gloves.

Coffee Break

We're now at an important juncture in the project, so before we continue, let's grab a cup of coffee and think about where we are.

- ❑ We made a sketch of the original floor.

- ❑ We ripped out the original floor and threw it in the trash.

- ❑ We took great care to dress up the entire hull/floor joint. It is completely free of debris and old chunks of filler.

- ❑ If the flotation foam was wet, we dug it out and threw it away, cleaned the bilge, *allowed it to dry*, and replaced the foam.

- ❑ We inspected all stringers and frames and replaced them where necessary. The top edges of the remaining substructure were cleaned and made ready to accept the new floor.

- ❑ The new floor pieces have been cut, fitted, and treated, and they now lean against the garage wall.

- ❑ Everything below floor level is clean, level, and *dry*.

- ❑ We read and reread the section on working with fiberglass, particularly the safety stuff.

- ❑ We're ready to put down the new floor.

Installing the New Floor

Begin the installation with the piece nearest the transom. Set it in place and mark the location of the stringers on the new floor piece so you know where to drive your screws when the time comes. Once you have it marked, slide it forward and out of your way. Now cut strips of fiberglass mat for the stringers and frames that fall under the first piece of floor. These strips should be wide enough to cover the top surfaces of the stringers and frames and hang over each side several inches.

Typically, there will be two stringers, one frame, and a small box around the drain plug under the first piece of floor. We want to be liberal with the resin, but we shouldn't need more than a pint for each piece of the floor. And, since there won't be a lot of cutting and fitting to fiddle around with, we can mix the resin "hot" for this job.

Once the resin is mixed, use your paint brush to completely coat the tops of the stringers and frames under the first piece of flooring. Immediately lay the strips of mat over the stringers and frames, then saturate the mat with more resin, using a brush or a roller. Be free with the resin, but don't slop so much on that it runs into the bilge cavity, where it may obstruct the flow of water through the bilge.

When the strips are in place, lay the new floor piece in position. With your power drill and 1¼-inch #8 stainless sheetmetal screws, screw it down, starting with the stringers (which will push any warps in the plywood to the outside) and spacing the screws about 8 to 12 inches apart.

Working your way forward, repeat this process until the entire floor is in place. When you're finished, you may notice a few places at the hull/floor joint where the edges of the plywood extend above the desired floor level. This usually occurs because of warped plywood. The high spots can be forced down by cutting some scrap lumber to a length equal to the distance between the desired floor level and the underside of the gunnels above. Wedge them in tightly where necessary and leave them in place until you've filled as much of the hull/floor joint as possible, and the filler has cured.

Figure 4-8. Braces between the new floor and gunnels will hold the floor flat until the filler around the edges cures.

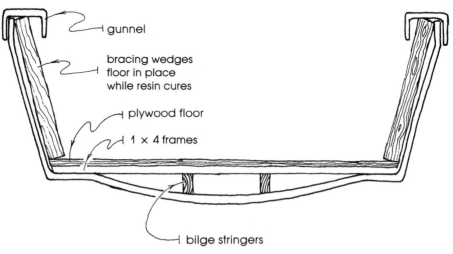

gunnel

bracing wedges floor in place while resin cures

plywood floor

1 × 4 frames

bilge stringers

Once you're satisfied that the floor is level, it's time to fill the joints, cracks, and any indentations in the plywood. You have a few options for fillers. Autobody fillers are readily available, generally inexpensive, easy to mix and work with, and quick drying. However, they *cannot* be used in any area where you expect constant moisture. In time, they will absorb water and disintegrate.

The second option is a flour-like product specially designed for thickening polyester resin, which is available in quart cans from such companies as Evercoat and Boat Armor. This stuff works well, but again there are disadvantages. As with resin and most other marine products—in fact, anything with a picture of a boat on it—it's expensive. Some are hard to mix thoroughly and require a high ratio of filler to resin.

I prefer a product called microballoons, which looks like finely ground Styrofoam (it's actually microscopic hollow balloons). It mixes well into a putty, it's easy to use, and it will never let you down. It's also relatively inexpensive (about $12 to $15 per pound, which goes a long way), but it may be a bit difficult to find. A retail marine store may not even know what it is. Again, check with fiberglass shops, or see the mail-order suppliers in Appendix B.

I'll take you through mixing filler with microballoons simply because it's my preference; there are adequate directions on the containers of the others. This stuff is silica based, which means that once inhaled, it tends to stay in the lungs. *Wear your dust mask when mixing.*

Uncatalyzed microballoon/resin paste will keep for several months in a tightly covered container; I use a 3-pound coffee can, which is about the right size and has a tight-sealing plastic lid. Fill the can about half full of resin (no catalyst yet) and pour in as much microballoons as will fit. You can mix the resin and balloons with a paint stick, but an inexpensive paint mixer chucked into your electric drill works much quicker.

Keep adding balloons and mixing until the stuff is slightly thicker than toothpaste. If you have large cracks to fill, you may want to mix it a bit thicker to keep it from running out of the joint. Once mixed to the desired consistency, put a glob on a clean piece of plywood or metal and add the catalyst. The mixing formula will be the same, with or without filler. Mix it well.

Use plastic spreaders (available from fiberglass suppliers and autobody shops) to push the filler into all the joints in the plywood, screw dents, the floor/transom joint, and the hull/floor joint that runs the length of the floor on each side. Allow it to cure until it's hard enough to grind, usually overnight.

When it has cured, grind any high spots away with a grinder, or an electric sander and 40-grit paper. You can also remove any braces that you may have used to keep the floor flat. At this point, the resin/filler fillet at the floor/hull joint will hold the floor securely in place.

Inspect the floor's entire outside perimeter carefully. If you failed to fill a joint or gap completely, the resin will run through the gap and into the bilge when you lay the fiberglass mat. That can get expensive.

Sheathing with Fiberglass

Now we can get the floor ready for a new coating of fiberglass. To ensure a sound bond between hull, transom, and floor, rough up an adjoining strip all the way around, about 6 to 8 inches up the sides of the hull, with a sander and 40-grit paper. Vacuum the new floor thoroughly, then wipe down the filler and adjoining surfaces with a rag dampened in acetone.

The fiberglass mat you bought should be rolled up, just as it came off the factory roll. To demonstrate, we'll use 60-inch-wide mat, which is commonly available and sufficient to span most boats this size.

As before, begin at the transom. Unroll the mat the entire length of the boat. Because the center of the boat is wider than the bow or stern, you won't have much surplus mat in the middle. On some boats, 60-inch mat may just cover the hull/floor joint. Trim the mat with scissors so that it extends all the way to the vertical sides of the hull; you want a uniform line the entire length. Roll the mat back up from bow to stern and leave it in the middle of the floor.

Now to mix resin. If you need another cup of coffee (or have already had too many and need to pump bilges), do it now: Once you start this, you'll have to stay right at it. Cut the top off a clean, dry, plastic milk jug, saving the handle. Put on your rubber gloves, fill the jug about three quarters full of resin, and add the catalyst. Again, the amount of catalyst you need will depend on the temperature and humidity to a certain degree. In this application, the resin can be mixed too hot. You want the resin to cure slowly so that it has time to saturate the plywood.

Once mixed, start at the transom and pour the resin on the first section of floor, spreading it evenly across the whole floor section with a paint brush or plastic spreader (still wearing your rubber gloves). Set the roll of mat against the transom and unroll it forward, making certain that it is straight and flat, just far enough to cover the first piece of floor.

Here you'll need a specialized tool, the fiberglass roller, which looks kind of like a paint roller with ridges. These are available made from throwaway plastic, or from aluminum, which can be cleaned in acetone and reused. Your marine dealer should have these, but if not check with the fiberglass shops or the sources in Appendix B.

Roll out the wrinkles in the mat into the corners. You'll find that the roller distributes the resin evenly and saturates the mat completely. You must avoid leaving the mat dry. Every fiber in the mat must be completely saturated with resin, which can happen only as a result of ample rolling and ample resin. As you work with the roller, and the resin begins to saturate the plywood and mat, dry spots will become obvious. Simply go back and add a bit more resin and roll it in.

When you've got the first section of floor down, you can unroll the remainder of the mat. The procedure from here on will depend on the design and size of the boat. In other words, don't paint yourself into the proverbial corner. If your boat is still sitting on the trailer, you won't be able to reach under the splash well at the transom or under a covered deck at the front of the boat. Plan it out so that you finish in an area where you can climb in and out without disturbing your work.

Work at a steady pace until the entire floor has been covered, mixing fresh resin as needed. When you're done, cut enough foot-wide strips of fiberglass cloth to run around the entire hull/floor joint. (Some builders used woven roving, identifiable by its characteristic large checkered pattern. If woven roving was used originally, then use it again instead of cloth.) These will run up into those areas of the hull you sanded earlier, covering and strengthening the joint between floor and hull, and tying everything together. Saturate the cloth and roll it in place just as you did the mat. If you have precut strips and can get to all the areas of the hull/floor joint, you can do this step at the same time as you lay the mat. If that isn't possible, allow the mat to dry until it's sandable, then rough it up with 40-grit paper, clean it with acetone, and apply the strips of cloth or roving.

When the resin has cured completely, sand or grind off all high spots or sharp points that may have appeared as the resin cured. We don't want sharp points under the new floor covering.

Inspect your work carefully. On most boats it is desirable to add an additional layer of woven roving at the corners of the transom and the transom/floor joint. The original designers considered these to be high-stress points; a little extra reinforcement here can't hurt.

Covering the Floor

You have two primary choices when considering the type of covering for your new floor; vinyl and carpet. Before the relatively new introduction of carpet in boats, the old standby had been vinyl. When you're out looking for a suitable candidate for rejuvenation, you'll see many older boats with this type of floor covering. Vinyl served its purpose well for many years and remains a viable option. However, it is difficult to lay because it tends to stretch, and it requires an absolutely flawless floor.

With those disadvantages in mind, I prefer to use marine carpet. Today's marine carpets are durable, easy to clean, oil and gas resistant, and usually made from ultraviolet-ray resistant olefin and polypropylene. Many lumberyards stock indoor-outdoor carpet and AstroTurf, intended for use around the home, but neither hold up in the marine environment.

Authentic marine carpet is much thicker and heavier than home-owner grade stuff. The best quality available weighs from 16 to 20 ounces per square yard, for the grass carpet, and 18 ounces for the plush style. Normally, plush carpet will cost about 10 percent more than grass carpet.

A prepackaged 6- by 20-foot roll of grass carpet may run as much as $150. Shop around; the markup is high. Many large marine dealers stock 6 × 100-foot rolls, and you can buy what you need at an enormous savings. Also check local carpet outlets to see if they have access to marine-grade carpet, and, if so, how much they'll charge. Auto upholstery shops may also use the plush carpet in vans and the trunks of cars. Check around. You'll be amazed at the wide variety of prices you hear, but be certain you are buying the right weight and true marine carpet.

The same shopping hints apply to carpet adhesive. Your local carpet shop buys in bulk and may agree to sell you enough for the project—2 to 3 gallons should do—at a substantial savings. Be sure to ask for exterior carpet adhesive.

You will need enough carpet to cover your floor and, in most cases, both sides of the hull. Lay out the carpet along the floor (the sides will be covered after the floor is down), much as you did the fiberglass mat. The floor piece should run all the way to the sides of the hull, and from the transom all the way forward. *Don't cut it too short.* The carpet can be cut or trimmed with a large pair of shears, or a sharp utility knife wielded from the back side.

At the transom there is a small, square hole in the floor that allows access to the drain plug. Be sure to cut a small "V" in the carpet at the corners of the cavity so that it will extend down into it.

Once the carpet is cut to size, pull it back from the transom and leave it in the middle of the floor. Now apply adhesive with a grooved trowel (1/4-inch grooves), only as far forward from the transom as you can reach. When the adhesive becomes tacky (usually several minutes; check the instructions on the can), unfold the carpet toward the transom, smoothing out the wrinkles as you go and rubbing the carpet into the adhesive (I use a small block of 2 × 4 for this). Be careful not to slide the carpet out of position when crawling over it.

When you've completed the first section next to the transom, pull the remaining carpet on top of it, and again apply the adhesive as far forward as you can reach. Roll the carpet forward and rub out the wrinkles. Continue the process all the way forward. You'll be able to work on the carpet as soon as it's down, providing you're careful not to put lateral pressure on it.

Use the same process for covering the sides of the hull. Measure from the floor up to the hull/deck joint and cut a single strip of carpet for each side of the boat. Use the same adhesive where possible. In some cases a can of spray adhesive (available in autoparts stores) will come in handy for areas under the gunnels and others that can't be reached with a trowel. It's expensive, so use it sparingly.

After the new carpet has set overnight, go back and trim away any threads at the seams. If you cut the carpet a little short in a few spots, now is the time to cut some filler strips and glue them in place with spray adhesive. The repair will never show—another advantage of covering your floor with carpet.

The Finishing Touches

Now it's time to solve two other problems that are primary causes of rotten floors. As I mentioned earlier, many floors rot from the bottom side. I have a theory why this happens. It seems that there is always a bit of water in the bilge. It may back up from the drain cavity or seep in from rain, but it always seems to be there. In the off-season, the best prevention is to keep the drain plug out and the bow blocked up high. That will allow any standing water in the bilge to drain out.

That doesn't solve the problem when the boat is in use, though. I think that any condensation or moisture remaining in the bilge ultimately will affect the bottom of the floor; the key to preventing damage is ventilation. As a matter of practice, I always install vents in my new floors. They should be placed on the centerline over the bilge channel, as far forward as you can get them and still keep them from underfoot and somewhat protected from splash and rain. The rest of the floor should be sealed off by the stringers. Your marine store will have a variety of locker vents designed to ventilate cabinets of larger boats. These serve nicely to cover a few 3/4-inch holes drilled through the floor. I'm convinced that it retards the rotting process.

When reinstalling the seats and other hardware that attaches to the floor, be sure to bed all screws properly. Coat them well with a good sealant, such as 3M-5200, Sikaflex, or even silicone (more on sealants and bedding compounds later). The objective is to keep water from seeping into the plywood laminates. If you follow these simple rules, I guarantee your new floor will far outlast the original.

THE HIGH POINTS

☐ Learn the basics of mixing resin and applying fiberglass.

☐ Read the safety cautions.

☐ *Pay attention* to the safety cautions. Really.

☐ Before tearing your boat apart, make a sketch of how it's put together, including all those things you'll have to remove.

☐ Make a materials list and shop wisely.

☐ Be methodical, patient, and *safe* when removing the floor.

☐ Check the flotation and replace if necessary.

☐ Check all stringers and frames for rot.

☐ Take special care to prepare the stringers, frames, and hull/floor joint to receive the new floor.

☐ Measure and fit the new plywood floor pieces; use your grinder to custom fit when necessary.

☐ Precut strips of mat to cover stringers and frames.

☐ Before screwing each piece in place, glass the tops of the stringers and frames.

☐ Check the hull/floor joint for high spots; brace them in place where needed.

☐ Fill all cracks, dents, and the hull/floor joint.

☐ Sand or grind excess filler and clean the surface.

☐ Cover the floor with marine-grade carpet, using exterior carpet adhesive.

☐ Install seats, accessories, and any interior panels that were removed; use a good sealant around the screws.

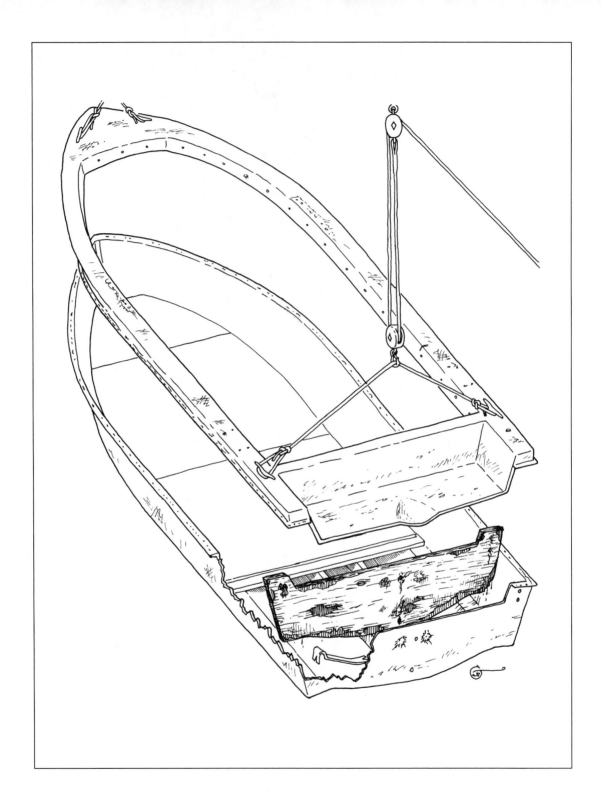

CHAPTER

5

Build a New
Improved Transom

When I ponder the "craftsmanship" that went into boats of this size, the transom represents one of my biggest aggravations. The floor, of course, is another. I can't point a finger at a single builder and say that their transom was worse than the next. In my estimation, they were all underbuilt. Some were better than others, but none were really adequate. And it would have been so easy to build them to last! Today, Ranger bassboats feature a solid fiberglass transom. 'bout time.

For the average person, the thought of replacing a bad transom is overwhelming. At first glance, your boat looks like one of those Fisher-Price toys that simply can't be taken apart. The fact is, these boats are put together by folks just like you and me. Sure, they've got some special tools that make the job easier, but you can work around those. Replacing a transom is a labor-intensive project, but if you've got the ambition and a little time, you'll probably be able to replace your transom for around $100—and have a product far superior to the original. So let's do it.

Separating Hull and Deck

If you discover a rotten transom during your survey, your first question will be, "How do I get to it?"

There are two approaches: You can lie on your stomach for a winter whacking it to pieces with a hammer and chisel—which means that the project probably will never get finished; or you can separate the hull and deck sections and replace the transom just as it was installed. This isn't nearly as difficult as it appears at first glance.

Boats of this vintage used one of only two types of hull/deck joints: the *shoe box* and the *flange* (see Figure 5-1). There were a few variations on these two themes, but I'll discuss them as we go. Both types of joints are covered by an aluminum extrusion, which forms part of the joint's integrity. In most cases the extrusion is molded to accept a rubber rubrail that surrounds the boat and protects the joint and the hull from scratches and dings. The surest method of determining which type of joint you have is to remove a stern corner cap; the joint will be clearly exposed and readily identifiable (see Figures 5-2 and 5-3).

Whichever type of joint you have, the procedure for removing the extrusion is much the same. Begin by removing the stainless screws on both corner caps and the bow cap; this will allow you to remove the rubber rubrail. Some builders used a single piece of rubrail that started at one stern corner and circled the entire boat to end at the other. Other builders cut the rubrail at the bow and covered the joint with the bow cap. You'll be able to tell which you have when you remove the caps.

You'll likely find the rubrail fastened with a single screw at the stern corners and perhaps one at the bow. Remove the screws and pry out one

Figure 5-1. The hull/deck joints are likely to be either shoebox (left) or flange (right). The shoebox joint is screwed or pop-riveted together, and covered by an aluminum extrusion. The flange joint is usually stapled together, with an aluminum extrusion screwed on. Rarely, flange joints are held together with a pressed-on extrusion (inset). I've seen this only on 1970s-era Crestliners.

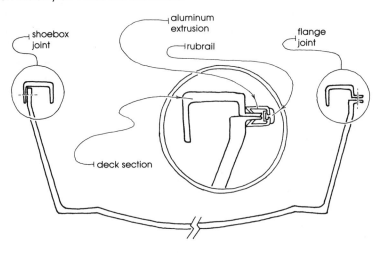

Figure 5-2. When you remove the stern corner cap, a flange hull/deck joint will look like this.

Figure 5-3. A shoebox joint will look like this.

end of the rubber with a screwdriver. Once you get it started, the entire piece should pull out easily.

I've come across one exception to this (there may be others), and it caused me trouble. Crestliner built a tri-hull in the early 1970s that used a unique extrusion pressed onto a flange joint, with no screws or rivets. To pry off the extrusion was to ruin it. Eventually I managed to get a new transom in the boat, but I had to do it from the inside—and I don't recommend that torture to anyone.

There's an easy way to tell if you have an oddball like this: Pull back 6 or 8 inches of the rubrail and check to see if the extrusion is fastened with screws or aluminum pop rivets. If it is, go on with the project. If it isn't, and you are intent on keeping the boat, you had better locate and price a whole new extrusion before you continue. That may be tough to do (although Wefco, one possible source, is listed in Appendix B). If you're shopping for a restoration project, I would simply avoid the oddball.

Once the caps and rubrail are off, you'll see the screws or pop rivets that attach the extrusion to the hull. As a general rule, pop rivets will be found only on a shoebox joint, and almost always on bassboats. The closely spaced rivets are usually $3/16 \times 1/2$ inch. Simply put a $3/16$-inch bit in your drill and drill them all out. Because they're aluminum, they'll come out easily, but be careful not to wobble the drill and widen the holes in the fiberglass. If that happens, you'll have to redrill those holes with an oversize bit and put in oversize rivets. Once the rivets are out, the aluminum extrusion will fall off.

If the extrusion is attached with screws (normally #6 stainless), you'll probably find that the standard screwdriver bits for your drill are too thick to fit inside the extrusion. To get around this, cut the shank off an old screwdriver with the correct-size head and chuck it in your reversible drill. Most of the screws will back out easily, but some may be stubborn. Take out all the easy ones first, then go back and start on the tough ones. Gently insert a pry bar between the extrusion and the joint and apply pressure, and they'll back right out.

When the extrusion is off, move to the transom and remove the extrusion that covers the hull/deck joint at the transom. Usually this is nothing more than a piece of light aluminum angle attached with a few screws, and it will come off easily. You'll also find a brass or plastic drain plug extending through the back side of the splash well. Take a flat-nose punch and pound downward on the flange until it breaks or collapses, then knock it out.

At this point, if you have a shoebox joint that was attached with rivets, you're almost ready to separate the hull and deck. If you have a flange joint, however, you have a bit left to do. You'll see that the fiberglass flange was stapled together every few inches. Yep. They all have to come out. The best method I've found is to grind off the tops with a small grinder and pull out the pieces with a pair of pliers. Be careful not to grind dings into the side of the deck section or through the flange. They can be repaired, but it only adds work.

On either design, at this point take a rubber hammer and tap under the joint all the way around the hull to loosen any bedding compound that may have been used to seal the joint. While tapping, slide a small pry bar between the joint and apply a little pressure. Usually, it will pop apart.

On flange joints, some builders put a bead of bedding compound between the flanges before they were stapled together. In most cases this compound has long since deteriorated, but there are often a few spots where it sticks stubbornly. In extreme cases you may have to slide the blade of your saber saw between the flanges and cut through the compound. It takes a steady hand, but it will cut easily.

Now comes the fun part. Once you're confident that the joint is free around the entire boat, tie a line through both bow cleats and both stern cleats and attach the lines to your hoist or block and tackle. Slowly raise the bow several inches until it's free; move to the stern and do the same thing. If you're going to have a problem, this is the most likely spot.

Occasionally, the underside of the splash well will be attached to the transom with a bit of bedding compound or resin. Crawl under the splash well and inspect where it meets the transom; the trouble spot should be obvious. I've also come across a few boats where the builders tied the splash well and transom together with a single layer of fiberglass mat. A keyhole saw (which has a flexible blade) will cut it without much trouble.

A similar problem may occur on the top of the transom where the deck section covers the transom. Again, a keyhole saw between the joint will cut away any old bedding compound. Keep a little pressure on these areas with your block and tackle; pry and tap them apart with a rubber hammer. I promise they'll come apart.

Once the hull and deck sections are free, hoist the deck section evenly, about 6 inches from the hull, and check it for sagging at the windshield. Some windshields are so heavy that the fiberglass might tear on each side of the deck as it hangs suspended between bow and stern. If this is the case, you have two choices: Remove the windshield or add a new lifting point.

If you have the ceiling height to lift the deck clear with the windshield still attached, I suggest that you run a 2 × 4 directly under the windshield across the boat, loop a rope from one end to the other, and tie another rope, from your tackle or hoist, to the loop. Now you can support the center of the deck section as you raise both ends. If you're planning to paint the boat, however, I suggest that you remove the windshield (see Chapter 6).

With the deck still about 6 inches above the hull, you're ready to disconnect the engine cables, wiring, and any plumbing. You'll also be able to see which systems stay with the hull, and which go aloft with the deck. Begin by cutting the wire ties that hold the wiring harness together, and trace all wires. Most will lead to the console and instruments. If you aren't an electrician, you'd better disconnect the wires one at a time and number both ends of each connection with a bit of masking tape. You'll save yourself some grief when it comes time to reconnect the harness.

If the boat has live wells or bilge pumps, simply disconnect the radiator clamps at one end of the hose. In most cases it will be easier to disconnect them at the through-hull fittings. If you're working on a bassboat with multiple live wells and bilge pumps, the systems can get a bit complicated. If you find yourself getting confused, draw a diagram or mark both ends as you did with the wiring. They're easy to take apart, but you have to remember how to put them back together.

The throttle/shift cable and steering cable usually stay with the deck section, depending on how the controls are mounted. In most cases the controls are screwed onto a piece of plywood that is in turn attached to the inside of the gunnel, which is part of the deck assembly. In the splash well, there will be a plastic ring or rubber boot designed to keep the cables from chafing. If you're planning to paint the deck section, you'll want to drill out the rivets that hold the rubber boot or ring in place and pull the throttle and shift cables out completely. Usually, the boots will be rotten and need replacing anyway.

The steering cable is much more rigid than the throttle cable; moreover, it can't be kinked and live to tell about it. As you slowly raise the deck section, you'll gain room to slide out the steering cable. Remember that you'll have to put it back in the same way. The alternative is to disconnect it at the helm—more unnecessary work.

At this point simply raise the deck section slowly and check to see that everything has been disconnected. Move the boat out from under the deck and find a spot to set the deck section. It will sit nicely on three sawhorses if you first nail a 2 × 4 across the top long enough to span the width of the deck. This will also be a good height to repair flanges, refinish dings and scratches, or what have you.

On paper this all seems like a terribly complicated project. The truth is that the entire separation can be accomplished in under two hours.

Removing the Old Transom

As with removing the old floor, removing an old, rotten transom is an imperfect science; unlike the floor, fortunately, it is much simpler.

You want to have your hull at a comfortable working height for this job. If your hull is still on the trailer and not on carts or a cradle, block up the trailer tongue until the rear of the trailer rests on the floor.

If your boat's floor was in good shape and didn't need replacing, and if the vinyl or carpet covering is intact and worth preserving, you'll have to take up the last 2 feet of carpet to repair the transom. If you're careful, you'll be able to get it back down, and any mistakes will remain unseen, under the splash well. If you've already replaced the floor, the section that meets the transom should have been left out, as discussed in Chapter 4. We'll proceed on the assumption that the old floor is still in.

Once you've pulled up the floor covering and rolled it forward, measure 24 inches forward on each side of the boat. Draw a line across and cut along it with your power saw, set to cut about ⅝ inch deep. You'll have to chisel out the last few inches on each side, where your saw can't reach. Use your grinder to grind around the edges until you can see the joint between the plywood floor and the hull and transom. Pry up that section of floor and throw it away.

The next step is the most important of the project. We have to try to determine the thickness of the original transom. If you build a new transom that is the slightest bit thicker than the original, the hull and deck sections will not line up when you try to put them back together.

The top edge of the transom is clearly visible; you'll be able to see the thickness of the fiberglass hull, the transom's plywood core, and the chopped fiberglass that covers the inside of the transom. You need to take

Figure 5-4. Top view of the edge of a typical plywood-core transom.

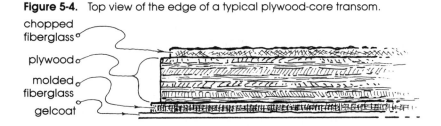

chopped fiberglass

plywood

molded fiberglass

gelcoat

the combined measurement of the plywood and its inside covering. *DO NOT* include the thickness of the hull.

This figure will range from about 1 1/4 inches to 2 1/2 inches, depending on the size of the boat. With your grinder, clean up the top edge of the transom, which normally is in pretty good shape. Measure the thickness to the nearest 1/16 inch in several places where the transom is in good condition, *and write it down*. Ideally, our new transom should be the exact thickness of the original, but because the new transom will be superior in construction, you can afford to let it be a tad thinner. *It cannot be any thicker*. I don't mean to be a nag, but this is important.

Next, grind the glass off the transom/hull joint on the inside, just as you did with the floor/hull joint, until the plywood is exposed. Generally speaking, if the plywood transom is rotten, it will come out relatively easily. Most of it will be delaminated to the point where you can pry it out with a pry bar, assisted by an old chisel in stubborn areas.

With your grinder, clean up the edges where the old ply was glassed to the hull, including any chunks of resin resulting from voids in the plywood that remain on the inside of the hull. As with the floor, you want a clean, flat surface to accept the new plywood transom.

If the plywood was extremely rotten, the lower legs of the outboard mounting bracket may actually have punctured the unsupported fiberglass of the hull. That will leave pieces of fiberglass protruding into the inside of the boat. Grind them off from the inside so that the back of the transom is flat and true. We'll repair the damage later.

Vacuum out your work area. Again, remember that resin will not adhere to wet or dirty surfaces. If the transom was in bad shape, the ply was probably wet. Set the boat in the sun for a day or two or clamp a couple of heat lamps in place to ensure that the surface is dry before you go on.

Installing the New Transom

For demonstration purposes, we will build a 1 3/4-inch-thick transom—fairly typical for boats like our generic 16-footer, but the procedure is the same, whatever the thickness of your transom. And we'll build a fiberglass laminated transom that will be far superior to the original.

The first step is to make a template of the transom, just as we did with the floor. Brown wrapping paper works well; if you have to tape a couple of pieces together, so be it. Tape a straight edge of the paper to the top straight edge of the hull. Push the excess into the corners and the bottom. If you do it firmly but carefully, you'll have an exact imprint of the inside of the hull at the stern. You can trim it inside the boat with a utility knife, or take it out and cut out the template along the hull lines with scissors. Either will work, but take care to get it as precise as possible.

Now we need to think about how to make our laminated transom the same thickness as the original. Our original transom was 1³/₄ inches thick. Two pieces of ³/₄-inch plywood will bring us to 1¹/₂ inches—¹/₄ inch short. Perfect. Add a layer of fiberglass mat—each netting about ¹/₁₆ inch thick—between the hull and the first piece of plywood, one between the two pieces of plywood, and one as a finish on the inside of the transom. Now, with 1¹/₂ inches of plywood and ³/₁₆ inch of fiberglass, we're only ¹/₁₆ inch shy of the mark—about right. You can always add another layer of mat to the inside if you feel you need the extra thickness.

Now you'll need two pieces of plywood the same size and shape as the template you cut. Again, you're faced with deciding what material to use. There's no mystery about what the factory used. Figure 5-5 shows a new transom that has just been installed in a new Larson. Although the factory gets their plywood in the precise thickness needed for each design, there's nothing special about it. AC-grade exterior plywood, which has fewer voids (voids will cause problems later) than cheaper grades like CDX, will work fine.

Mark around your template on both pieces of plywood and cut out the transoms with your saber saw. Custom fit them to the hull as necessary with your grinder. Now cut off ¹/₈ inch of the straight top edge of the transom pieces. We're going to glass the top edge solid to prevent water from getting to the laminates and avoid the fate that befell the water-logged and rotten original.

Before we begin to install the first piece of ply, some other wrinkles may need ironing out first. If the transom has been weak for some time, the back of the hull has probably lost its shape. With the rotten transom out, you may notice that the hull's top edge bows out a bit. When you install the new transom, you'll want to pull it back into shape as best you can. That requires a little ingenuity, and if you can come up with a better method than mine, by all means use it.

Set your first piece of ply in place and check for gaps between it and the hull. These are the areas that you'll have to pull together. In most cases the worst areas will be down the center of the transom. Figure 5-6 shows the back of a typical transom and the holes that are normally present to accommodate the towing eyes and two drain plugs.

Clamp the top edge of the ply to the hull with wood clamps or C-clamps and drill out the towing-eye holes on each side (usually ³/₈ inch in diameter). With the same bit, drill a hole in the center of each drain plug.

Figure 5-5. Here's the plywood transom core bonded into the hull.

Insert ³/₈-inch bolts in each hole, using flat washers on the inside, and tighten them down. Check to see if the hull has been pulled snugly to the ply. If you're lucky, it has.

If not, find a couple of pieces of angle iron long enough to extend the height of the transom. On each piece of angle, mark and drill holes that coincide with those that you drilled in the drain plugs. Bolt them in place with one on the outside and one on the inside. Again, check for gaps.

Figure 5-6. To straighten a bowed transom, bolt on an angle iron using the splash-well and bilge drain holes. Put enough tension on the line to pull the transom straight and leave it in place until the resin cures on the new plywood.

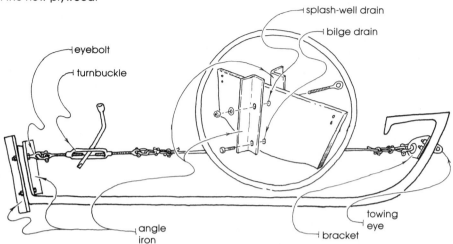

splash-well drain

bilge drain

eyebolt

turnbuckle

angle
iron

bracket

towing
eye

Usually, this will pull the new ply and the hull together. Okay, so a couple of you are still standing around scratching your heads and saying, "That didn't do it, wise guy. Now what?"

There shouldn't be more than one or two places in the hull's lower corners still causing you problems. From the outside, drill ³/₈-inch holes through the hull and the ply and insert bolts where you need them (don't overdo it). Satisfied? We'll fix the holes in your boat later.

Once you've got this system figured out, take it all apart, set the second piece of ply in place, and clamp both to the hull. Drill matching holes in the new piece.

In very rare cases, even two pieces of ³/₄-inch ply won't take the bow out of the back of the hull, even though you have pulled them together every place possible. In these boats, it may simply be impossible to bring the hull back to its original shape. You may have to live with it, but there is one more trick that just may solve the problem.

With the bracing system bolted in place, move down the inside piece of angle iron to the top drain plug. Replace the ³/₈-inch bolt with a ³/₈-inch eyebolt, leaving the eye to the inside. Now go forward to where the bow eye extends into the boat. Some will have one shank, and others two. In either case, fashion a piece of metal that you can bolt onto the shanks that will provide you with a point to hook a small cable to. Now you can run a small cable (or rope) from the bow to the eyebolt in the transom, inserting a small turnbuckle on the transom end. This will allow you to snug the entire transom assembly forward a bit while the resin cures, and often solve the worst cases.

Now it's time to put it all together. Cut two pieces of fiberglass mat that conform to the inside of the transom, much as you did with the paper template, with enough extra material (several inches) on each side to extend out onto the sides of the hull. Cover all the holes on the outside of the hull with small pieces of duct tape, cutting small slits in the center of the tape to admit the bolts. The tape will seal around the bolts and help minimize the amount of resin that runs out of the holes.

Now coat the inside of the transom with catalyzed resin and put the first piece of mat in place. Saturate it with resin and roll it flat and into the corners. Set the first piece of ply in place and add the second piece of mat, using ample resin. Set the second piece of ply in place, making sure that both pieces are aligned as they were when you drilled your holes.

If you haven't mixed your resin too hot, you should have ample time to jockey the pieces into place, but don't dally. This is no time for a coffee break. Once you're satisfied that the new pieces of ply are in place, clamp the top edges together with wood clamps or C-clamps so that there are no gaps, then insert the ³/₈-inch bolts through the drain-plug holes that you drilled.

Grab your drill and Phillips bit and a handful of 1¹/₄-inch #10 stainless sheetmetal screws and screw the two pieces of ply together. Don't worry about a pattern. The objective is to take out all gaps or voids between the two pieces of ply.

If you're fixing a bowed transom, bolt on the angle iron and install all the bolts you had planned for earlier. If a cable run forward is necessary to pull the bow out of the transom, now is the time, but be careful not to pull the transom too far forward. It should be straight across the outside of the hull. *Now* take a coffee break.

While you're drinking your coffee, inspect your work carefully. This is the last chance you'll get to make final adjustments and push the mat into the corners where the transom and hull meet. When you're satisfied, put your fiberglass roller and any other tools that were in contact with resin in a can of acetone, and let the resin cure for 24 hours.

Now you can disassemble the bracing system. The bolts that were used to pull the assembly together have been glassed in place, but once the nuts are removed you'll be able to pound them out easily from the inside. Remove the duct tape from the outside of the hull. No doubt some resin oozed out of the holes and ran down the hull, but once cured you can gently scrape it off with a sharp chisel. Cover every hole with new pieces of tape so the holes won't leak when you put on the final layer of mat.

Remember, you cut the ply ¹/₈ inch shorter than the hull. Grind the top edge of the new plywood transom clean. Do the same to the inside corners where the new mat and ply meet the hull. Remove all ragged pieces of resin or mat with your grinder so you can get a smooth finish with the final layer of mat. Fill any gaps at the top or around the sides with your mixture of resin and microballoons so that you have a flat surface everywhere. Once it cures, grind off the rough edges and clean the adjacent areas of the hull with acetone.

The transom is now ready to be finished, with two primary objectives: It must be structurally sound—sufficient to withstand the weight and torque of the motor—and it should look good. To ensure its strength, the transom must be securely glassed to the sides of the hull, using woven roving, mat, or cloth. Your best bet is to use whatever was used by the factory, which should be evident when you inspect the sides of the hull at the transom joint. If you have any doubt, use at least one layer of woven roving, which will be far superior in strength to mat or cloth.

Cut a strip of roving about a foot wide and long enough to cover the entire joint between the hull and new transom—6 inches on the hull and 6 on the transom. Don't be concerned about thickness at the corners as long as the fiberglass doesn't extend onto the transom where the splash well and the transom meet. The additional thickness of roving behind the splash well will prevent the deck from sliding back to its original position. Dry-fit the roving, then coat the hull and transom where this reinforcing strip goes with catalyzed resin, stick the strip of roving in place, wet it out with resin, roll out any air bubbles, and allow it to cure.

The final layer of fiberglass can be either mat or cloth. Cloth will provide a smoother finish, but I prefer mat because it provides a thicker layer of glass. Before you make the decision, check the thickness of the new transom in the center. We wanted our transom to be 1 3/4 inches thick. So far we've installed two pieces of 3/4-inch plywood and two pieces of mat, for a total of about 1 5/8 inches. This means that the finish layer can't exceed 1/8 inch.

Cut the finish layer, still using your paper template so that it wraps around the corners a few inches, just as you did with the first two pieces of mat. It must also extend into the bottom of the hull several inches and over the top edge of the transom. Apply it as you did the other layers, bearing in mind that every time you grind or sand a layer of fiberglass, it must be dry and cleaned with acetone before you try to apply another layer. *All* surfaces must be clean and dust-free.

When the final layer has cured, sand the entire surface with 80-grit paper and clean it with acetone. Don't reinstall the floor until the bottom drain plug has been installed, which is discussed below.

There should be a minimum of six holes in the back of your boat—two in each upper corner to accommodate the towing eyes, one in the center toward the top for the splash-well drain, and one directly below it for the bilge drain. The towing-eye shanks, usually 3/8-inch diameter, can simply be drilled out from the outside. If the eyes show signs of wear or bending, replace them. You can find replacements at any well-stocked marine store.

Before you install them, think about why floors and transoms rot. It's simple: Water was allowed to reach the plywood's laminates. So before installing the towing eyes, drain plugs, and outboard bolts, fill all the holes with a good marine sealant. Silicone caulking will suffice for the towing eyes; use plenty and bolt the eyes in place. For the bottom drain you'll want something with better adhesive properties, such as 3M-5200 or Sikaflex. Both should be available at your marine store.

In most cases the bottom drain is a 1 × 3-inch brass tube, available at most marine stores or suppliers. If you recall, you drilled a 3/8-inch hole through the center of the drain plug if you built a bracing system to cure a bowed transom. Enlarge the hole with a 1-inch auger or chipper bit; note the hole's slight upward angle and tilt your drill perpendicular to the angle of the transom.

If you look at the drain tube, you'll notice that one end has a finished flange and the other doesn't. You want the finished end to the outside. Insert the tube from the outside, then reach around inside the transom and mark the tube about 1/8 inch longer than the thickness of the transom. Again, note the slight angle. Pull it out and cut it off with a hacksaw, then clean off the burrs with a file.

Installing the tube can be clumsy. A friendly boat shop may loan you a flanging tool; if not, you'll have to bend over the inside flange with a punch and hammer. If you don't have enough room to do this inside the boat, you'll have no choice but to put the finished flange on the inside and bend over the flange on the outside. If you're careful, it won't look too rough. Remember to use plenty of sealant.

Don't do anything with the top drain. That will have to wait until the deck is back in place.

There may be other holes in the transom to deal with. If an outboard was bolted on, simply drill out the holes, using the holes through the hull as a guide. If you're changing outboards, the old holes will have to be filled with resin and microballoons, and new ones drilled.

If you had to make a couple of extra holes to pull the hull and transom together, you'll notice that they're partially or completely filled with resin from the three layers of mat. Fill them the rest of the way with resin and microballoon paste. When it has cured, carefully grind out a small dish approximately 1 inch larger than the original hole and no more than $1/16$ inch deep to provide adequate purchase for a layer of surface filler. Be sure to wipe down the area with acetone.

Companies such as Boat Armor make polyester surface fillers that are inexpensive and easy to use when repairing small dings or scratches. They are generally white; if your hull is white, this filler should work pretty well, although it may not provide a perfect color match. If you're planning to paint the boat, it doesn't matter. If you can't live with the slight difference in color or if your hull is a color other than white, you'll have to try matching the gelcoat.

I consider matching gelcoat an art; it's the reason there are a few good glass men around who earn more than the governor of Minnesota. Any marine store will sell you a gelcoat repair kit containing a small can of gelcoat and hardener and several small tubes of pigments. The object is to mix the colors and perfectly match the color of your boat. Then, the directions say, add a couple of drops of hardener, fill the hole, cover it with a small piece of waxed paper, let it cure, and presto! Your problems are solved.

Well, maybe it's just me, but I've tried that process more times than I can count, and I've never been satisfied with the results. Matching a new, bright gelcoat is tough enough, let alone one faded by 15 years of sun. It never looks the same in the bright sun as it did in the shop. And if you apply too little filler, you'll have to repeat the process, with another chance of missing the color; too much, and you have to try to sand it down with 600-grit wet/dry sandpaper without sanding out the shine of the surrounding area. Depending on the temperature and humidity, the gelcoat filler may not cure well under the waxed paper. And if your boat has a metalflake finish—well, you've got more problems. In short, I'm not the guy to tell you how to use a gelcoat repair kit. I'd rather paint the whole boat.

Fortunately for me, this book assumes a total renovation, and that includes a whole new paint job. I've seen few boats of this vintage that didn't have enough scratches and dings to warrant the time, effort, and expense. But in the event you don't want to undertake a full paint job, or even if you do, I have another trick left up my sleeve.

As a matter of practice, I always cover the area where the outboard mounts with a piece of aluminum outside the hull and one inside the splash well. And no, I don't do it *just* to avoid matching the gelcoat in

Figure 5-7. Adding a piece of aluminum outside the hull and one inside the splash well where you mount the outboard will prevent damage to your new transom.

areas where I've filled holes. As you snoop through boatyards, you'll see plenty of older boats with neat little rings punched through the top of the transom by outboard brackets. I can't see any reason to spend time and money building a new transom and then wreck it like that—and that kind of damage is inevitable. I don't find the aluminum unattractive, and it's certainly practical. Some builders have even started installing it on new boats.

If you plan your new transom installation carefully, most if not all repairs can be kept under the piece of aluminum. Usually, a piece 12 × 12 inches by .090 thick (any sheetmetal shop will cut you a couple of pieces) will cover all repairs and protect the transom. The actual length will depend on the outboard mounting brackets. You can't put it on yet, but you can draw an outline on the outside of the hull and plan to make most if not all your repairs within the outline.

In extreme cases of rot, the outboard mounting brackets may have poked right through the hull itself. If you recall, you ground off the rough edges from the inside before you installed the first piece of ply. The new plywood transom will give you a sound, flat base from which to repair the outside. This will be a cosmetic repair, and it too should be covered by the aluminum transom guard. (The actual repair procedure is discussed in Chapter 6.)

At this point the only project left before reattaching hull and deck is replacing the piece of floor you removed to gain access to the bottom of the transom. Do it as described in Chapter 4, keeping in mind that you want to completely seal the bilge and the joints where the floor meets the transom and the hull. As with the corners, add a strip of roving along the floor/transom joint to reinforce this critical area.

Painting the inside of the transom is optional. In most boats you'll have to look hard to see this area. Pettit and Interlux both make inexpensive utility paints, easy to apply with brush or roller, that are suitable for this application.

I've never had a problem with shoebox joints, but if your boat has a flange joint, now is the time to inspect it; a few spots likely will need repair. Grind away "rotten" or rough fiberglass around the area. When it's clean, wipe it down with acetone. Tape a piece of cardboard to the flange's bottom; insert a small piece of waxed paper between the cardboard and the repair so the cardboard will release, then run a piece of masking tape onto the finished areas around the repair so you don't slop resin where you don't want it. Fill the area with scraps of mat and resin. When they've cured, sand them smooth and level using a sanding block with 80-grit paper. Remember: The repaired areas will have to match the original flange to accept the aluminum extrusion. You won't need to

Figure 5-8. Tape cardboard covered with waxed paper on the underside of the damage. Carefully clean up the edges and repair the flange, following the instructions given in Chapter 6.

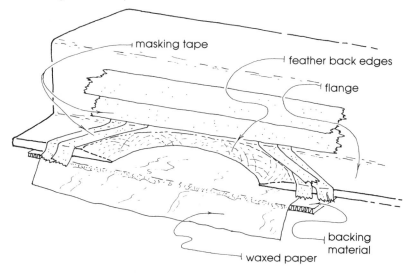

worry about a perfect finish here; these areas will be covered by the flange.

Now the transom is in place, with the top completely sealed. The boat is clean, and you're satisfied. Right?

Reattaching the Hull and Deck

At this stage, the shoebox joint is ready to go back together, but if your boat has a flange joint, you'll have to sand the adjoining surfaces of the flange on both the hull and deck sections with 80-grit paper. Make sure the flanges come together smoothly. There may be areas where old bedding compound will have to be ground off.

On certain designs, some builders installed a narrow piece of 1/4-inch plywood all the way around the hull to serve as a backing plate and provide purchase for rivets or screws. I've never found a rotten one, but it's possible. If so, cut out the bad spots, grind the hull smooth, coat new pieces with resin, and clamp them until the resin cures.

Move the deck section over the hull and lower it into place. With one exception, there is no reason why it shouldn't fit like a glove. The bow sections should fit together perfectly, and the holes in both sections should line up, *if you haven't made your transom too thick*. Guess who had to learn this lesson the hard way.

If you've spent an hour walking around the boat swearing under your breath and drinking coffee (or stronger) because the deck section won't fit over your new transom, put down the coffee (or whatever), grab a marking pen, and crawl inside the boat.

Draw a rough outline of the splash well on the transom, then raise the deck section high enough to give you room to work. Inspect the back of the splash well for leftover bedding compound or fiberglass, which may be keeping the deck and hull from sliding together. If you're lucky enough to find some, grind them off and try fitting the deck again.

If that wasn't the problem, measure the thickness of your transom. So it's too thick; you wanted it strong, didn't you? Grind out the area within the splash well's outline until you think you've gone far enough. Although it shouldn't be necessary, don't be afraid to grind into the plywood. Because your new transom is laminated fiberglass, it is far superior to the original, and you shouldn't have to go too far. Grind until the deck fits as it should and there is enough room between the transom and the splash well to add a layer of mat to the repair.

Now. The deck section fits. It almost looks like a boat again.

You'll want to add a bead of marine sealant between the flanges of a flange joint, just as they did at the factory. Use something like 3M-5200 or Sikaflex for their superior adhesion qualities. Both are a bit expensive (about $8 a tube). If you have microballoon paste left, it will also work, but keep in mind that you'll have to apply the paste and fasten the extrusion before it cures. You may need some help for this.

Fasten the extrusion using new rivets or screws just as you took it apart. It should give you no difficulty at all.

Attach the rubber rubrail in one corner and insert it into the extrusion. They are usually a bit stiff, and you'll probably have to use a screwdriver to push it in all the way around the boat. If you start at the stern corner, it may also be necessary to stretch it a bit as you move forward. You can judge how much by checking the total length every few feet. If the rubrail has been cut and you would like to replace it, I've listed some suppliers in Appendix B. I'm sure there are others, so check with your local dealer.

Those of you with flange joints are wondering why we haven't replaced the staples that joined the flanges. Without an expensive tool and some expensive staples, this just isn't possible for the do-it-yourselfer. With the proper adhesive sealant, I also don't think it's necessary, in *most* cases. Eliminating a structural feature the factory felt necessary is a tough decision to make. However, the products I mentioned above not only offer excellent adhesion, but they also flex, which eliminates much of the shock this joint receives. Have faith in better living through chemistry.

If the flanges and the extrusion are in good condition and all the screws tighten snugly, that should be good enough. I've come across a few where the extrusion was a bit sloppy and some of the screws didn't seem to take. I wasn't satisfied and again, I designed my own solution.

The inside of the hull/deck joint is visible in most boats. In those cases where I felt it needed additional strength, I roughed up the joint with 80-grit paper, wiped it all down with acetone, and added a strip of woven roving. In effect, I glassed the two sections together every place I could access. You'll probably never have to take them apart again, and even if it becomes necessary, the strip can be easily cut. Do whatever makes you comfortable.

You're ready to reconnect the wiring and any other hardware that was disconnected when you took the two sections apart. It's also time to install the aluminum pads and the splash-well drain. Start by drilling the 1-inch hole for the drain, just as you did with the bilge drain. Again, take note of the slight angle when drilling.

When the hole is drilled, attach the piece of angle that came off the top rear of the transom. Be sure to bed all the screws with silicone. Next, put the outside piece of aluminum plate in place, with the splash-well drain directly in its center, and clamp it with wood clamps. Mark the drain plug from the inside as well as any outboard mounting holes you may have, and drill them out.

Drill about three holes on each side of the plate and one in the bottom center that will accept a #8 or #10 stainless screw. Clamp it back in place and drill small pilot holes where the pad will attach. Also, mark each edge on the top of the transom so you can align the inside piece of aluminum. This must be the same width as the outside piece, and the height must fit comfortably in the splash well. Mark the inside piece and drill out the drain hole as you did with the outside piece of aluminum. A single mounting hole in each corner will suffice.

Mount both pieces on the transom, making sure to run a bead of silicone around the perimeter where you have drilled the mounting holes.

There is one caution to remember when adding the aluminum guard

Figure 5-9. When installing the aluminum pads and splash-well drain, make sure that the inside and outside pieces of aluminum are the same width and that the height fits comfortably in the splash well.

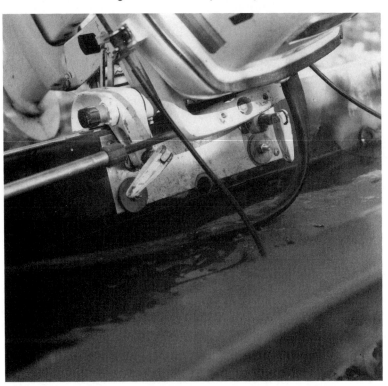

to your new transom. Outboard mounting screws only open so far, and not all outboards are the same. Back out the ones on yours all the way and measure the distance. That's how thick your transom can be. Although I've recommended that you use aluminum .090 thick, if you have to go thinner, do it. Two thin pieces will be better than nothing.

The last project is the installation of the splash-well drain tube. Perko, for example, makes a two-piece, snap-together plastic drain tube that works nicely in the splash well. Your marine dealer should have them in stock. Install it according to the directions, making sure that you use ample sealant. This is a likely spot for water to enter the plywood laminates.

Now the job is done, and you have a better transom than the original.

Again, don't make a snap decision to forget the project simply because all this sounds so complicated. Explaining how to replace a transom is much like cooking a good meal; it's usually much more enjoyable to do than it is to explain.

Read the chapter, then go out and take a look at your boat. Pull off a couple of feet of rubrail and check the joint. Crawl inside and look over the area where the splash well and the transom meet. Look at the inside corners of the transom. Inspect the severity of the damage on the outside.

I promise that, as you get into the project, it will all make sense.

A QUICK REVIEW

- ❑ Remove the corner caps, rubrail, and the aluminum extrusion.
- ❑ Remove any rivets or screws attaching the hull/deck joint.
- ❑ Grind off the staples securing a flange joint.
- ❑ Knock out the drain tube in the splash well.
- ❑ Carefully separate the joint with a rubber hammer.
- ❑ Slowly lift the deck section; disconnect wiring, plumbing, and steering cables.
- ❑ Set the deck section aside, making sure that it is well supported under the windshield.
- ❑ Grind the top edge of the transom clean.
- ❑ *Accurately* measure the thickness of the plywood core, including the inside finish layer of fiberglass. Jot it down!
- ❑ Pull up the floor covering and remove 2 feet of the floor.

- ❏ Remove the lower drain plug and towing eyes.

- ❏ Grind the chopped fiberglass away from the inside corners of the transom where the plywood core meets the hull.

- ❏ Remove the plywood core, using a pry bar, hammer and chisel—whatever it takes.

- ❏ Grind the inside surface of the hull clean and smooth wherever the new ply meets the hull.

- ❏ Cut out paper templates delineating the new transom core's shape.

- ❏ Cut as many pieces of plywood as necessary to match the original thickness—*less ³/₁₆ inch*. You'll add three layers of mat, at ¹/₁₆ inch each.

- ❏ If the hull at the stern is bowed, design a system to pull it back into shape, flush with the new plywood transom core.

- ❏ Make sure the hull is clean and dry.

- ❏ Install the first layer of mat, then the first piece of plywood, followed by the second layer of mat and the second piece of plywood. Make sure everything is in place as you planned, then let it cure.

- ❏ Clean up all the corners between the new core and the hull with your grinder.

- ❏ Fill any gaps in the corners and the top with a mixture of resin and microballoons.

- ❏ Apply a reinforcing strip of woven roving all the way around the corners, where the hull meets the transom.

- ❏ Clean the corners with acetone and apply the finish layer of mat, making sure to seal the top edge of the plywood core completely.

- ❏ Sand the new transom smooth with 80-grit paper and paint if desired.

- ❏ Replace the floor and covering as you removed it.

- ❏ Put the hull and deck back together as you took them apart.

- ❏ For flange joints, add a bead of sealant between the flanges. If you feel the need, (do you wear a belt *and* suspenders?), add a few strips of fiberglass to the inside of the joint.

❏ For shoebox joints, add a strip of sealant where the hull and deck sections meet.

❏ Repair any damage to the outside of the hull.

❏ Add aluminum plates to protect your new transom from the outboard brackets.

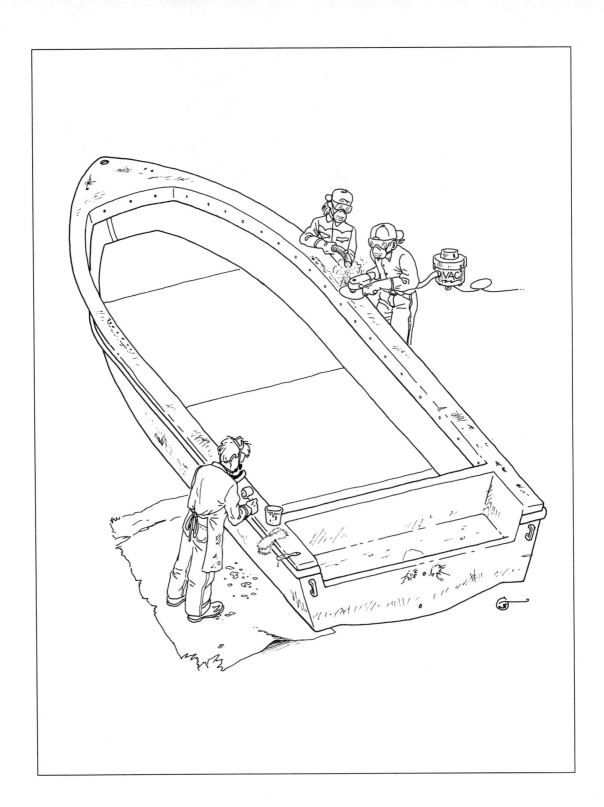

6

The Narrow Path to a Gleaming Finish

In the last chapter I discussed briefly my feelings on the nearly impossible task of trying to match gelcoat color with a patch kit. From the day your boat comes out of the mold, it begins changing color. Sure, for the first few years the fading is subtle, and you can get away with a few patch jobs. But as it ages, the fading progresses, the dings and scratches accumulate, and finally it reaches the point where a complete paint job is the only feasible solution.

A good paint job is no longer out of reach for the do-it-yourselfer, but there are many options you'll have to consider, as we'll discuss shortly. But regardless of what paint and application procedure you decide on, the important first step is surface preparation.

Preparation: The Key Ingredient

Early on I suggested that you avoid boats with severe structural damage; in most cases, they're just too tricky and expensive to repair. Minor damage, which you're much more likely to encounter, and which can be repaired readily by the determined runabout renovator, falls into four basic categories: surface scratches that don't penetrate the gelcoat; a gouge that goes through the gelcoat and well into the fiberglass laminates; that mysterious pest commonly referred to as crazing; and, less commonly found, small holes through the hull or deck.

Some damage is difficult to categorize, but variations or combinations

Figure 6-1. Your renovation likely will include repairing surface scratches like these.

Figure 6-2. Repairing a gouge that exposes the laminate will be more difficult.

Figure 6-3. Crazing is probably the most common gelcoat problem you'll encounter.

of the basic repair procedures for the four general types of damage should take care of almost anything you're likely to encounter.

Before we discuss each type of repair in detail, there are a few basic rules that must be followed when making any of these repairs:

❏ The area to be repaired must be ground or sanded to remove chips of gelcoat or ''rotten'' fiberglass.

❏ The repair and the area around it must be dusted and cleaned with acetone.

❏ All surfaces must be absolutely dry before applying resin or filler.

Repairing Gelcoat Scratches

The most common damage—and fortunately the easiest to repair—is a minor scratch in the gelcoat. Although the procedure sounds complex, once you've repaired one successfully, you'll find that you can fly through the rest—and you'll learn a great deal about fiberglass repairs in general.

To get started, put some 80-grit paper on your orbital sander and make a pass or two over the scratch. Keep the sander flat; your only objective here is to clean dirt and scum from the area. The cleaning will also help to define the edges of the actual scratch. Now, tilt your sander and run the edge of the sanding pad into the scratch. One or two passes, tilted each way, should clean the scratch all the way to the bottom. If you rub your finger over the scratch, you'll notice that you've created a small "dish" that radiates outward from the scratch. This process is often referred to as *feathering*, and you'll use it on every type of repair—the deeper or wider the scratch, the wider the dish. A $^1/_{16}$-inch-wide scratch, for instance, might be feathered back so that the final repair is 1 to 1$^1/_2$ inches wide. The goal is to provide more surface for the filler to adhere to, and remove sharp edges to ensure that it stays put.

When you're finished sanding, wipe the area with acetone and apply masking tape around the scratch, making sure to stay outside the feathered area.

With practice you'll be able to skip the taping process, but on your first few repair attempts it serves two purposes: It keeps you from slopping filler all over the boat, which you'll have to sand off later, and it serves as a gauge for judging the thickness of the filler. So for now, run masking tape around the edges of the dish.

For minor scratches like this, I suggest that you make it easy on yourself: Boat Armor (and others) makes a quick-drying, easy-sanding, polyester-based filler, available in small cans with its own hardener, that will spread into the scratch with few, if any, air bubbles.

Spread the filler into the dished-out scratch with a plastic spreader or putty knife to the same thickness as the masking tape, or even a little higher depending on the depth of the scratch. The filler will shrink as it cures; the deeper the scratch, the more it will shrink. When the filler dries, pull off the tape.

Figure 6-4. Grind a gradual taper surrounding dings in the gelcoat, fill, and sand flush.

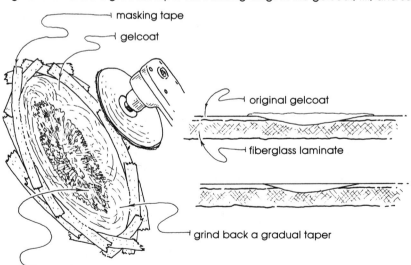

The final step is sanding the filler smooth and flush with the surrounding area. This is no time to be in a hurry; how well you sand determines how well your repaired area will look. Don't sand the filler with an air or electric sander on your first few attempts; you can undo all your work with a careless flick of the wrist. Sand the repair with a rubber sanding block and 80-grit paper, keeping the block flat, until you begin to see the outline of the dish. Then change to 120-grit paper and hand-sand the repair until it is flat and consistent with the surrounding area. Done.

Repairing Gouges

Gouges, which for definition's sake are just deep scratches, are repaired much the same way, with an added wrinkle: If the damage has been there for some time, the fiberglass cloth or mat likely is frayed and ''rotten'' on the edges. No, fiberglass doesn't rot in the same sense that wood does, but once it's been gouged and torn, the fibers become chalky looking and will not accept new resin or filler. You'll have to grind this back until you find good fiberglass. Consequently, a 1/4-inch gouge can easily turn into a 2- or 3-inch-wide repair.

You can dish out or feather the gouge much more quickly with a small grinder than with a sander, but keep in mind that runabout hulls aren't very thick, especially on the sides. If you're not adept at using your little grinder or are momentarily inattentive, you may grind right through the side of the boat. If there is any doubt in your mind, stick to your sander and either 80- or 40-grit paper. Once you get the gouge dished out, tape it off as before.

The type of filler you use depends on the depth and width of the damage. As a rule, a narrow gouge that has only destroyed a single layer of fiberglass cloth can be filled with a mixture of resin and microballoons (which won't shrink and crack in a deep repair), using the same procedures as filling a scratch with polyester filler. Because you'll be working with larger quantities of filler, you may want to add a piece of masking paper under the area to be repaired to keep resin from slopping onto the boat, particularly if you're working on a vertical surface. The microballoon mixture will probably have a few air bubbles in it when it cures. Sand it down and apply a finish coat of polyester filler to fill the holes, then finish it off as directed above.

An extremely deep gouge may need to be reinforced with a strip of fiberglass mat. When dishing out a deep repair, use 40-grit paper to roughen the surface and provide extra adhesion. Using a small paint brush, coat the area with resin, then lay in a piece of mat cut to fit. Saturate the mat with resin and roll it in place with your roller. When it cures, grind (if you're adept) or sand it down flush with the surrounding surface. Clean the area with acetone, apply a skim coat of polyester filler, and finish sand with 120-grit paper.

Deep gouges are often found on the bow stem and the keel, where the gelcoat has worn off over years of beaching and ramming the dock. You may have to dish the repair as much as a foot on either side of the keel. Hold off repairing this area until you've gained a little confidence with the smaller repairs.

Curing Crazing

Repairing crazed areas is tough at best. As I said earlier, if you're not prepared to live with at least a few of these ubiquitous blemishes, avoid boats with truly bad cases.

Usually, crazing appears as a series of crooked, horizontal lines or as a star pattern. Treat each *set* of cracks as a single gelcoat scratch. That means that when you dish them out, you may have a repair area several inches in diameter. Because the cracks are seldom deep, the area can be filled with polyester filler, but it's hard to achieve a flat, level surface on a large area using an orbital sander. Depending on the size of the repair, it's better to file down the bulk of the filler with a small wood rasp or an autobody rasp. With practice, you'll be able to match the original hull or deck form. Do the finish sanding with a flat rubber sanding block.

Figure 6-5. A wood rasp or an autobody rasp will make shaping and smoothing repaired areas easier. A flat rubber sanding block is ideal for finish sanding.

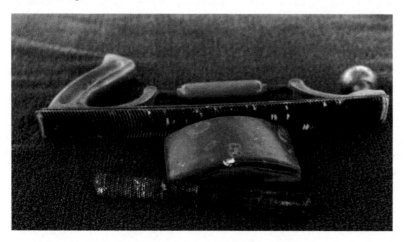

Holes aren't all that common—at least in boats worth renovating—but you may encounter a few small ones. A severe dent may have to be treated as a hole. In fact, you may have to cut out the dent or grind off the back side and create a hole in order to repair it properly. It's rare to find a hole below floor level because this part of the hull is generally much thicker than areas above the waterline.

A hole above floor level will be covered on the inside with carpet or upholstery, which will have to be stripped away from the area. From the outside, grind the area around the damage until the rotten fiberglass disappears. If you're getting handy with the small grinder, feather the edges with that; if not, stick to your sander and 40-grit paper. There is no hard-and-fast formula here, but if you have a hole 3 inches in diameter, you'll need to feather the edges back at least an inch or two to expose enough new fiberglass for your repair to adhere to.

As we saw when repairing holes in the transom, a hole must be covered on the inside to provide a solid surface on which to build the fiberglass repair. On the transom, we used the new piece of plywood. For curved areas of the hull, we can use a piece of cardboard taped to the inside. Large holes on a flat surface can be backed up with a piece of plywood braced in place with scrap lumber. Whichever you use, add a piece of waxed paper to the face of the backing to keep the resin from sticking to it.

Figure 6-6. Duplicate the original laminate schedule when patching. For maximum strength, the new layers should overlap the old and be carried up the ground-in slope surrounding the hole. (Reprinted from Allan H. Vaitses, *The Fiberglass Boat Repair Manual.*)

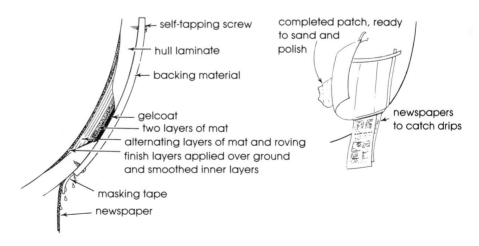

Inspect the area closely to determine the extent of the damage in all directions, then mark around the area with a pencil. Get inside the boat and pull down whatever covering there is over the area, then drill a few small holes around the area from the outside to define its extent. On the inside, grind or sand the area several inches beyond the holes that you drilled. Clean the area with acetone and apply a single layer of woven roving to the inside. Because the roving will serve only as a backing plate, the area that spans the hole does not need an excess of resin. Simply saturate it enough to allow the roving to firm up when it cures.

After it has cured, start grinding out the damaged area from the outside, being sure to feather it back 2 or 3 inches around the edges. You'll know you've gone far enough when you begin to see the new roving.

Damage this severe usually means that you'll have to add a layer of cloth between two layers of mat as you lay in the repair. The mat provides the thickness and the cloth the strength. Start with a layer of mat next to your roving and roll in any subsequent layers needed, making each piece slightly larger than the last until you have covered the feathered area. They can all be applied at once; just make sure to saturate them well with resin and roll out the air bubbles.

Spread microballoon paste topped with polyester filler—as with any other surface repair—reattach the carpet or whatever finish covered the inside, and you're done.

These repairs sound much more difficult than they really are. If you start on the bottom of the boat, where your learning curve won't show, you'll be a master by the time you get to the more visible areas or severe damage on the sides, transom, and deck.

Preparing the Surface for Painting

By the time you've repaired the scratches and dings, you'll have a pretty good idea of what's necessary to prepare the remainder of the boat for painting. Every area that you intend to paint must be sanded carefully. Sanding serves two purposes: It cleans the surface of dirt, water stains, and scum; and it leaves small scratches in the gelcoat that ensure the adhesion of the paint or primer.

Before you get out your sander, strip all the hardware—cleats, step pads, light fixtures, etc.—from the deck. In most cases, this is as quick as trying to mask around such irregularly shaped objects. In addition, it's common to find crazed areas around deck hardware. With the hardware removed, they'll be much easier to repair.

Remove the seats, side panels, and the like from the interior. It's also a good idea to disconnect the instruments and remove them from the console (be sure to mark the connections). Usually, the instruments have a single post on the back side that tightens a bracket against the inside of the console. They'll come out easily.

The windshield is tough to mask, and even tougher to paint around. Most windshields are attached with studs that ride in a channel on the bottom piece of the frame. If you crawl under the console you'll see the studs and nuts. Take them all off and lift the windshield straight up. Now you're ready to sand.

You can use your orbital sander on the flat surfaces, making certain that you keep the sanding pad flat. Resist the temptation to tilt the pad to clean up stubborn areas. Inevitably, you'll leave behind a small dish in the gelcoat that you might not see until it's painted. You'll see it then, I assure you. You'll have to sand the inside and outside corners by hand to avoid taking off the edges.

What grit paper you'll use will depend on what type of paint or coating system you select (more on this below). If you've decided to prime the boat with a sandable primer before painting, you can sand the gelcoat with 120-grit paper, followed by 220-grit to sand the primer. If you're using a paint that doesn't require a primer, then you'll have to use 220-grit from the start. Be sure to go over all of your repairs carefully. A thick, sandable primer will fill 80- or 120-grit scratches, but most paints won't—something you may not notice until you're all done painting.

Finally, give the whole boat a good cleaning. If you have a drain nearby, wash off all the sanding dust with a hose and a soft rag. Once the dust is washed off, give the entire surface a close check with a good light. If you miss a single spot, the paint will start to peel right there.

Paint: Sorting Through the Options

Selecting what paint to use for the old tub may be the most befuddling task in the entire renovation. There are literally dozens of products available, and some are extremely complex.

There is no way that I can suggest the right brand or type of paint for everyone to use on every boat and in every situation. Your final selection will depend on the boat, the size of your wallet, your workspace, your abilities, and your access to tools and equipment.

Although I can't offer many "do's," I can offer a couple of firm "don'ts":

Don't haul your boat over to your friend-the-mechanic's house or the local body shop to have a coat of acrylic enamel sprayed on your fiberglass boat. The standard argument goes, "Ya, it's good stuff; they use it on fiberglass cars." True, but do you know of a Corvette that is constantly exposed to the amount of water, sun, and abuse that most boats receive? Within a few seasons you'll become unpleasantly aware that you wasted your time and cash.

Don't let someone talk you into shooting a new gelcoat. This requires a well-equipped expert to apply successfully, and it usually isn't cost effective for boats this size.

Don't even consider a metalflake finish. First, successful application is way beyond the average do-it-yourselfer. And as I said earlier, the metal flakes also absorb ultraviolet rays from the sun, resulting in severe fading of the horizontal surfaces. If you've been wandering through boatyards, you've seen boats so afflicted.

Don't confuse a metallic finish with metalflake, though. I've used metallic finishes many times with good results (although it works well only when you're spraying-on the finish). Because the flakes are much smaller than those in a typical metalflake, they come mixed in the paint and they can be applied through a standard nozzle. However, it is not a common option in marine paints that can be brushed or rolled.

Now that we have the "don'ts" out of the way, I can try to help you make some sense of the complex coating systems on the market today. When you understand your options, you should be able to make your own decisions based on the variables.

Before you even begin to research the types of paints available, you'll have to decide how you'll apply it—spray, or brush and roll. I don't recommend spraying for the average do-it-yourselfer. In the first place, you probably don't have the kind of workspace that will allow you to do it safely and efficiently. You'll also need some fairly sophisticated equipment; your electric house sprayer from Sears won't work. And you'll need experience. A successful spray job demands a sound understanding of sprayers and nozzles and regulators and working pressures, as well as a sharp eye and a steady hand—which only come from experience.

Even for those few who have ample experience spraying cars or machinery, you'll find that many marine paints differ in unique ways from the traditional coatings you're used to—and you're still probably faced with an inadequate workspace.

Besides, that's why the marine industry developed paints that can produce high-quality finishes with a brush and roller.

Without going into a lengthy and meaningless discussion on the complex chemistry of modern marine paints, suffice it to say that they fall into three broad categories: epoxies, alkyds, and urethanes. Each type is chemically unique and intended for specific applications. Epoxies are extremely durable, expensive, and probably overkill on boats of this size. Alkyds, usually considered as a deck paint, are cheap and fairly easy to apply, but I don't recommend them as the single paint on boats of this size.

My choice is a urethane-based paint, which provides a durability and quality of finish that an acrylic or alkyd enamel simply cannot match. Some manufacturers refer to their products as polyester urethanes, and others as polyurethanes. Unless you aspire to wear a lab coat at Dow Chemical, a knowledge of the practical differences between the two is useless. Just call it a matter of semantics and trademarks, and we'll call them all urethanes, as they are all urethane based. Unlike conventional paints, they don't dry by solvent evaporation, but *cure* with the addition of a catalyst, like polyester resin.

One of the best examples of this type of paint is a two-part urethane (a polyester urethane, semantics lovers) called Awlgrip. This is an extremely durable paint, and probably the closest thing to a new gelcoat available. This complex coating system, which uses a variety of cleaners, primers, reducers, and converters, can be applied to steel, aluminum, wood, or fiberglass, each using its own set of procedures.

As with most marine-related subjects, there are trade-offs. Although cheaper than a new gelcoat, Awlgrip and other two-part urethanes are very expensive. They are also extremely toxic. The manufacturers make no bones about telling you just what will happen to you if you don't follow the safety procedures. Awlgrip and its ilk are also very, very hard, which means, like gelcoat, it's difficult to touch up a scratched surface. Accept the fact that you'll have to live with new dings until you have so many that it's obviously time to repaint. With care, though, that will be many, many years. It's up for argument, but I think Awlgrip is the best boat paint available; I use it almost exclusively in my shop, with not a single complaint.

The other predominant brand of urethane-based (a polyurethane, if you're keeping score) paint you'll hear about in the boatyards is DuPont Imron. Unfortunately, it can be applied only by spraying, and is intended for professional application. But for those of you who may want to do the surface preparation and take your boat to a body shop for paint, it's a good choice. (Look for a body shop specializing in painting big trucks. Imron is very popular for long-lasting custom paint jobs.)

Of course there are other brands of urethane paint (including Pettit's Dura Thane, a two-part urethane specially formulated for brush-and-roller application; even Sherwin-Williams makes a urethane-based marine paint), but the two above are the ones found most often in boatyards. These two-part urethanes are considered hi-tech and a bit mysterious by the average do-it-yourselfer. Because of the cost, complexity, and the hazards of application, you may decide to look for something a little less intimidating.

There are many other options available, which I'll call "shelf paints," because you'll find them sitting on the shelves of every well-stocked marine store. The first thing you'll notice when you start shopping is that nearly everyone stocks Interlux and Pettit (although there are many other brands). The next thing you'll notice is that you have a severe headache. On the Pettit shelf you'll see cans labeled Easypoxy, Unepoxy, Polypoxy, Shipendec, and others. On the Interlux shelf you'll see such names as Interthane Plus (another two-part polyurethane), Topside, Brightside, and Deck and Striping enamels. It goes on and on.

There was a time when I was convinced that these people's only motive in all this was to confuse me. But the truth is, each of these products is designed for a specific application. On my 20-foot sailboat, I've rolled Interlux Micron 33 on the bottom as antifouling, brushed on Pettit Dura Thane for the waterline stripe, and sprayed Awlgrip above the waterline.

A paint job for the average 16-foot runabout doesn't need to be that complicated. The average user is looking for one paint that will do the entire job, and for that one paint I heartily recommend that you stick with a urethane-based paint. It will provide a high degree of durability and a glossy finish anywhere on the boat. Most are relatively easy to use and require no special tools or skills. Just read *and follow* the instructions on the can.

As with most decisions in a renovation project, the key is education. Find someone in your local shop who knows paints and applications and see what he suggests for your particular boat. Study the different types of paints, and their intended uses and applications. When you've studied the available options, you'll be able to make an informed decision about one of the most important aspects of the job: to prime or not to prime.

Priming will just about double the expense and effort of a paint job. On the other hand, if you don't do it when you should have, you may have to do the job all over again. That will be *four* times the expense and effort.

If you've made extensive repairs that have left raw fiberglass exposed, most manufacturers will insist that you prime to ensure that the paint adheres adequately. A good layer of sandable primer will expose to view, and may even fill, minor scratches that have been left behind.

So, the definitive answer to the question to prime or not to prime is that there is no definitive answer. It all depends on the extent of your repairs and your final selection in paint. When possible, do it.

Another bit of solid advice. If your can of paint recommends that you use XYZ surface prep or ABC reducer or MNO primer, use it. Don't try to cut corners and substitute another brand or product. Most of these products are parts of a complex system. Each material and step of the project depends on the last, and most are chemically dependent on one another.

Also give some thought to color selection. Because of color coordination with the interior, some of you won't have much choice, but keep in mind that white is by far the easiest color to maintain—and it goes with everything. As I mentioned earlier, darker colors on horizontal surfaces are exposed to the relentless assault of direct sunlight; sooner rather than later, they'll fade.

Applying the Paint

There are just a few things left to do before applying the paint. The first is to wipe down the entire surface to be painted with the surface prep recommended by the manufacturer, exactly according to the directions on the can.

Next, mask off those areas that you don't want painted. That may include any deck hardware you didn't remove, the rubrail, or a second color on the hull.

Masking is something of an art, but it's another one of those jobs that you'll get good at with a little practice. Take your time. A good masking job is critical to achieving a satisfactory finish, and there are a few tips to make it easier.

First, be sure to buy a high-grade masking tape, preferably one made especially for painting. The paper-thin masking tape available at the five-

Figure 6-7. This type of stripe creates a bit of extra work when you're painting the hull. Mask off the stripe and paint the hull; then mask off the hull and paint the stripe (see Figure 6-8).

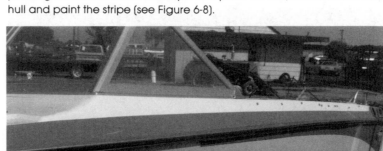

and-dime will allow paint to bleed under it, and will cause you plenty of trouble when it comes time to pull it off without damaging your new paint.

Stick to a width of ¾ inch. Unlike wider tape, it will bend around corners without wrinkling. There is no point in putting more tape on the boat than necessary. To be effective, any tape must be firmly put in place. Rub down all the edges firmly and carefully with your fingers.

If your boat has a stripe, such as the one in Figure 6-7, you'll have to mask it off, paint the hull, then mask the hull and paint the stripe. The edge where the two colors meet must be sharp and clean. You'll find a thin, plastic masking tape at your local autoparts store specially designed for this purpose. Apply tape to the edge first, then tape paper to the tape. Beware of masking with newspaper. A glob of paint may bleed through newspaper onto your new paint underneath. Pick up some heavy brown paper at the local autoparts store.

Unless accent and waterline stripes are more than 2 inches wide, I don't recommend painting them at all. A good marine store will have an array of high-tech tapes, in a variety of widths, colors, and patterns, that will replace this time-consuming job. Carefully applied, they'll look as good as paint, and are easily replaced. In fact, you may want to enliven

Figure 6-8. Using special plastic masking tape and heavy brown paper, tape the edge first, then tape paper to the tape. Avoid using newspaper for this; the paint may bleed through.

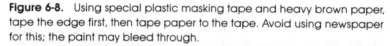

Figure 6-9. Save yourself time and money: Use high-tech striping tape instead of painting on accent and waterline stripes that are less than 2 inches wide.

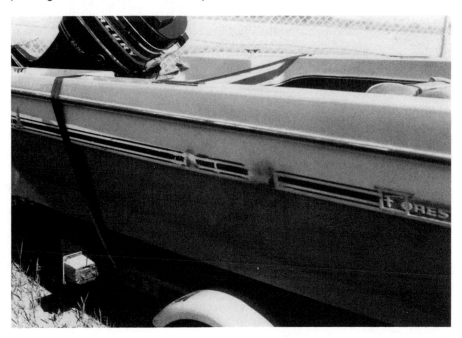

the appearance of a plain-Jane boat by adding an accent stripe where there was none.

Now that we've cleaned the hull and done any masking we need to take care of, we're ready to paint—almost. The last step, just before painting, is to wipe down the entire surface again with whatever the manufacturer recommends.

I've already suggested that you avoid trying to spray your boat. There are just too many *expensive* risks involved for the average do-it-yourselfer. However, if you are set on a sprayed finish, do the repairs and surface prep and take your boat to the body shop ready to paint. Stick to a well-known product like Imron, and be sure to find a shop experienced with it.

Even though two-part urethanes are designed for the do-it-yourselfer, they too can be tricky to apply. The good news is that every manufacturer will provide precise instructions, including such things as the proper temperature range for application, number and thickness of coats, surface preparation procedures, and precise mixing instructions. Do *exactly* what they tell you, and you can't go wrong.

Most urethanes will eat a normal brush or roller, so you'll probably be directed to use a badger-hair brush and either a foam or nap roller designed specifically for urethane paints. If you can't find these locally, see Appendix B.

Most manufacturers also suggest that applying urethane paints is a two-person job. Working shoulder to shoulder, the first rolls on the paint, concentrating on even coverage and the recommended mil thickness. If you don't know what a ''mil'' is, don't panic. If the manufacturer recommends the first coat be 2 to 3 mils thick, go to the lumberyard and look at a piece of 2- or 4-mil plastic. Also consider that at 2 to 3 mils they're allowing you about a 33 percent margin of error. However, most will suggest multiple thin coats instead of a single thick coat. *Don't cheat!*

The second member of the team should be right behind the one with the roller. His job is to smooth out the overlap marks that will be left by the roller with his badger-hair brush. He too must be concerned with thickness and most manufacturers will offer their own techniques that may include the use of two brushes and, perhaps, a thinner.

I know I've harped on this before, but I can't stress it enough. Study the mixing and application procedures of the paint you've selected and follow them to the letter. This is the only way, and I mean *the only way*, that you'll achieve a satisfactory finish.

A final reminder on the work area. Most of you won't have a dust-free booth to use on paint day. Although a little dust in your finish won't be a complete disaster, try to keep it to a minimum. Pick a day when there is little or no wind and put a window fan on the downwind (even if there is no wind) side of your shop to keep the air turned over in the work area. Vacuum the shop area well; then, if possible, dampen the floor a bit with a hose just before you start, being careful not to spray your prepared surface. This will keep the fan (and your feet) from stirring up any remaining dust. *And while you're painting, wear your respirator.*

Summary

I realize that I've been a bit vague in this chapter, but I think the reason should be obvious. I could write an entire book on the application of every brand and type of paint that's available today, and the truth is that much of the text would come right off the cans and tech manuals. Read them all and read them carefully.

For the absolute novice, I can offer one final bit of advice. If you've replaced your floor and transom, you've already made a considerable investment in time and money. At this point it would be a shame to jump headfirst into the painting project and end up with a cheesy paint job.

As I explained earlier, I got started in the repair business out of necessity. I never took a course in fiberglass repair or painting. I had a small fleet of 8-foot rental sailboats that had been used like bumper cars for three years—and they needed repairs. They turned into experiments. I could sand one and prepare the surface in half an hour. I intentionally put deep gouges in a couple just to see if I could fix them. I've still got one that is painted with maroon Awlgrip on one side and bright blue Imron on the other.

Practice, practice, practice.

If you've made the commitment to do the entire project yourself, you can adopt the same approach. If you live in the Great White North as I do, junk snowmobile hoods make excellent practice projects. If you snoop around, you can probably find one for nothing. Old boats, golf carts, and fiberglass lawn furniture also work well to learn on. Find an old junker and fix it. If you're not satisfied with the results, put a few gouges in it, sand it off, and fix it again. The cost will be minimal, and the experience that you gain will be invaluable. By the time you're satisfied with your work, you'll know how to mix resin, apply fiberglass, work with fillers, prepare the surface, and apply the paint.

And it's fun!

TOWARD A PERFECT FINISH

❏ Before applying any repair material, the surfaces must be clean and dry.

❏ Practice mixing resin.

❏ Learn the proper technique of feathering.

❏ Sand your repairs carefully, making sure they're smooth and flat.

❏ Sand the entire boat with 220-grit paper to clean and etch the surface, ensuring paint adhesion.

❏ Research and study paints and their applications.

❏ Make sure your work area is in proper order before you paint.

❏ Avoid acrylic enamels, new gelcoats, and metalflake finishes.

❏ Unless you're absolutely certain that you and your work area are up to it, don't attempt to spray your own boat.

❏ FOLLOW THE INSTRUCTIONS ON THE CAN!

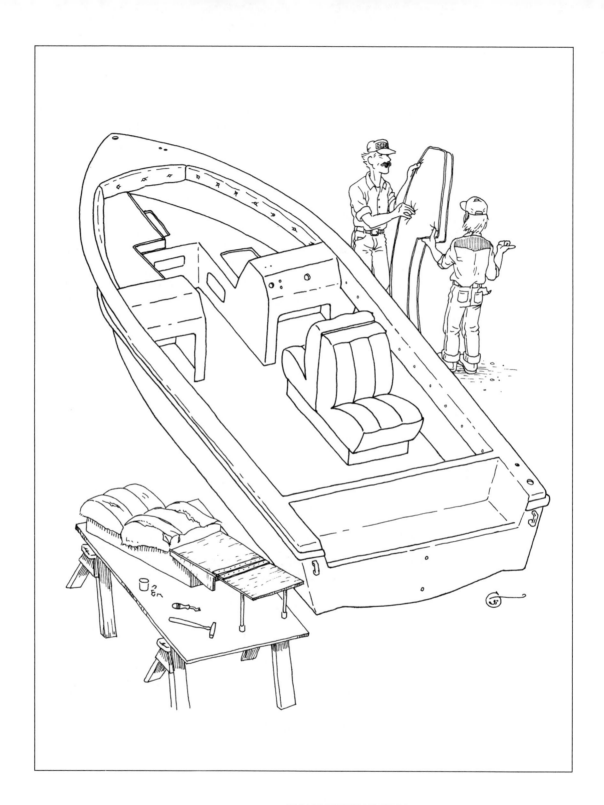

New Life
for Old Interiors

S̲o your boat is sitting in the garage
with a new floor, a new transom, and a shiny new coat of paint. It's looking pretty good, and you're getting antsy and want to go boating. Unfortunately—or fortunately, depending on how much you're enjoying this
project—you've probably got some work left to do.

If your boat needed a new floor and transom, it probably needs new
upholstery, too. Even if it isn't shredded, it'll be so brittle and faded that it
will disgrace your new paint and carpet. Besides, the seat bases, backs,
and bottoms are probably rotten and need replacing anyway. Of course
you already knew that from your survey, right?

The Upholsterer's Apprentice

I'll assume that no one has a commercial sewing machine and the expertise to replace their own upholstery. If you do, you can teach me. The best
most of us can hope for is to save a few bucks by doing as much of the
replacement as we can. Labor is expensive; there are savings to be had
with a little sweat equity.

You can save yourself some cash by carefully removing all of the staples and the individual pieces of upholstery and taking them to the shop.
Careful: If they're in bad shape they'll be brittle and tear easily. You want
them intact.

Keep in mind that if you're dealing with a pair of lounge seats like the one in Figure 7-1, you have four bottoms and four backs that are identical. You only need to salvage one good pattern from the bottom and one from the back for the upholsterer. The same applies with multiple pedestal seats. On bassboats and open-bow boats, there may be several different designs and shapes of cushions. Be sure to catch them all.

When you've removed the upholstery, you'll find that the foam cushions are covered by a light piece of plastic. This is intended to shed water that may seep through the seams of the upholstery. If it's torn or worn, don't forget to have it included in your estimate.

The last thing you'll want to check before heading off to the upholstery shop is the foam itself. Today's builders use essentially the same basic foam used for flotation, modified to allow it to be heat-molded to the desired shape. Seat foam is nearly indestructible and seldom requires replacement, but if yours is bad, it can be replaced with a firm polyurethane foam, available in most department or fabric stores in a variety of shapes and sizes. Simply copy the existing patterns and cut the new foam with a sharp utility knife or an electric carving knife accordingly.

Figure 7-1. A complete runabout renovation almost certainly will include reupholstering the lounge seats.

Figure 7-2. Once the individual pieces of material have been sewn together, simply staple them to the plywood backs or bottoms.

Now you're ready to start shopping for sewing bids. As I said early on, this can be one of the most expensive portions of the renovation, so spend some time shopping around. The final cost will depend on the number of cushions, the hourly labor rate, and the type of material you select. Obviously, you have no control over the number of cushions you need. You also have only limited control over the type of material you buy.

No material will stand up to prolonged exposure to the sun. But all things considered, one of the most practical and durable materials available today for the average runabout owner is expanded vinyl, which resists ultraviolet rays well. Other, more exotic materials are available, but they are generally too expensive for boats this size.

Let your fingers do the walking and phone every upholstery shop in your area. Make sure they have access to marine materials and experience in working with them. Don't discount the auto upholsterer; many do fine work, but make certain when you ask for estimates that everyone is quoting the same materials. Don't try to compare apples to oranges.

You have more control over the final variable, the labor rate. Get on the phone and call around. You'll find a wide range of rates, but beware: Cheaper isn't always better. At each shop, ask to see samples of their work. Take in every piece that you need done and get a written estimate, making sure that they have access to the material you selected, and that they're using Dacron thread, which will hold up to the sun's assault.

While the upholstery's in the shop, you can rebuild any rotten seat bottoms, backs, or bases. Regardless of the builder or type of seat, most are constructed of 1/2- or 3/4-inch plywood. That's handy; you should have some scraps, already treated with wood preservative, left over from the floor or transom. Replacement is pretty straightforward. Just use your old pieces to make patterns for the new. I've never found one that was shot to the point where I couldn't take a pattern.

There is a caution, though: If you have a pair of lounge seats, take one apart and rebuild it completely, keeping one intact for reference. Some of the old hardware that allowed the seats to pull flat is a little confusing.

When you've got one torn apart and the new pieces cut, there are a few things you can do to improve on the original design and ensure that your repair job will last.

I said it before, and I'll say it again: Never put anything back together with staples when you can replace them with stainless sheetmetal screws. The typical lounge-seat base—just two sides and two ends stapled together into a box—is a good example. Three 1-inch #8 screws in each corner will be far superior to the staples used originally. And before you

Figure 7-3. Rebuilding lounge seats can be a challenge. Take one apart and put it together again, just to be sure you can do it.

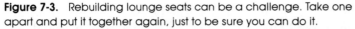

screw the pieces together, mix up a cup of resin and seal the edges of the plywood and glue the corners of the base together.

Now round off the corners a bit with your grinder so they won't snag your new covering. If you haven't already done it, give them two coats of wood preservative, then give the corners, top edges, and bottom edges another coat of resin. If you're the extra-careful type, let them cure for about an hour and give them another coat.

Cover the bases of lounge seats with the same carpet and adhesive you used on the floor. Cut a piece of carpet equal to the height of the base and glue it on. To hide the seam, position it so it faces the hull.

Another improvement you can make to some lounge or pedestal seats while they are apart and before you put on the new upholstery is to fit them with better-quality hinges. Most pedestal seats are hinged on each side so the backs can be folded down to the bottoms. Generally, the hinges have either three or five screws in each side. At first glance you'd think more is better. Not so. In most cases, five screws indicate that the hinges are attached with ¹/₂-inch #10 *wood* screws. Once the wood has been wet awhile, those five screws start to let go. The wood only has to be wet, not rotten.

Hinges attached with three screws are probably put together using *machine* screws, and a handy little item called a *wood nut*. For long life, install all hinges using wood nuts (you can find them at an industrial fas-

Figure 7-4. This pedestal seat would benefit from better-quality hinges. Plan to improve on some hinge designs when you restore the seats.

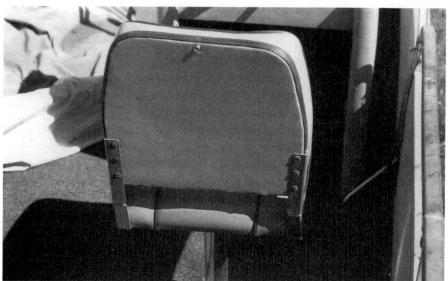

Figure 7-5. Use wood nuts, available from industrial fastener outlets, when you reinstall the hinges.

Figure 7-6. Reassemble the seats just as they came apart (except use wood nuts and stainless steel screws). Don't forget the plastic moisture barrier between foam and vinyl covering.

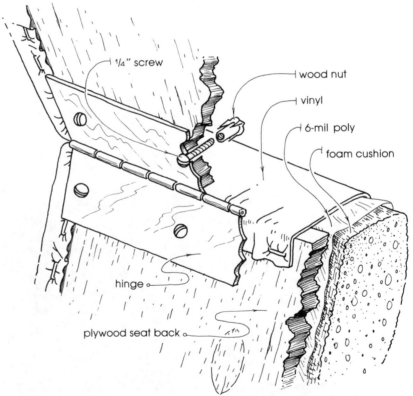

tener outlet), including the three sets of hinges on a lounge seat.

Set the hinges against the back or bottom pieces, just as they were positioned before, and mark the holes. If your original hinge had five holes, you only need to mark one on each end and one in the center. Remove the hinge and drill out the holes to $^{19}/_{64}$ inch, which is the size needed to accept a $^1/_4$-inch wood nut.

The machine screw must go through the hinge first, just as the wood screw does. Start the wood nut with a tap from the opposite side of the plywood, then put a small bead of silicone around the shaft of the wood nut and pound it down until it's flush. When it comes time to screw in the $^1/_4$-inch stainless machine screws, put a good bead of silicone under the edges of the hinge to keep out water.

Before you attach the new upholstery, give all the exposed plywood two coats of a good utility or bilge paint. If you feel like going the extra step and don't mind a little mixing, use a two-part epoxy paint. It will last much longer and is only slightly more expensive than a utility paint. The idea is to seal the plywood completely. Two coats of wood preservative and sealing the edges with resin are mandatory. A good coat of epoxy paint is the perfect finishing touch.

Attaching the New Upholstery

There is no secret to this job. If you took good patterns to the upholstery shop and you cut the new backs and bottoms accurately, the new upholstery should slip easily over the new plywood. Don't forget to line the insides of the new pieces of upholstery with plastic waterproofing, leaving it long enough to cover the bottom or back edges.

Don't settle for anything less than Monel staples, or they'll rust within a few seasons. Your marine store or upholstery shop should have them. You want $^1/_4$- to $^3/_8$-inch staples. If you have chosen a very heavy upholstery they can be as long as $^1/_2$ inch, but don't buy them any longer than necessary to penetrate the fabric and bury in the wood backing. A common electric or hand stapler will do the job.

Start stapling on one long side, concentrating on the straight edge, with the staples approximately 1 inch in from the edge of the plywood. When you have one side finished, move to the opposite side, gently pulling the upholstery over the cushions until the upholstery seams line up with the plywood. Do the other two straight edges the same way, saving the corners until last.

Look at the old upholstery and note how the corners were tucked—the excess material was folded over itself to keep the wrinkles from showing on the seat corners. When you've tucked one, the rest will come easy. After you finish stapling everything in place, trim off any excess upholstery and plastic.

Figure 7-7. If you replace upholstery, make the effort to replace all of it, including upholstered side panels.

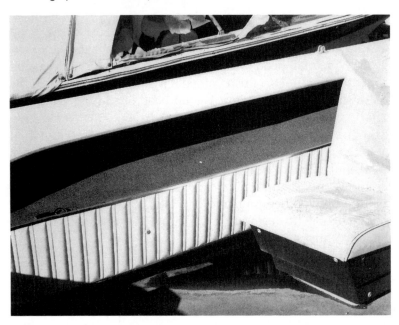

Don't Leave the Job Half Done

As I mentioned earlier, your boat may have other upholstery beyond the seats. Usually, boats of this type have upholstered side panels; there may also be a piece at the top of the splash well, or upholstered doors covering the storage area beneath it (Figures 4-3 and 7-7). In any case, these are all repaired exactly the same as the seats. Be sure to check the thickness of the plywood, though: In most cases it will be ¼ or ⅜ inch thick, instead of the ½-inch ply used for the seats.

I don't particularly care for the type of splash-well cover shown in 4-3, typical of the old tri-hull Chryslers and a few other builders. It looks cheap, but it's an expensive piece of upholstery that is subject to all sorts of abuse in this location. These pieces usually snap to a piece of wood screwed to the floor, which is a real toe-stubber, and usually gets beat up from moving gas cans and batteries in and out of the storage area. Before long, the upholstered panel looks like it's been through the wars.

If you're interested in making some improvements, this is a good place to start. After all, now that you have all-new carpeting, you don't want a ratty-looking splash-well cover spoiling the effect. You're better off removing it and installing a trim piece, like the one shown in Figure 4-3.

Measure the length and width of the fiberglass surrounding the inside

Figure 7-8. An upholstered door covering the storage area under the splash well is another prime candidate for new upholstery.

of the splash well, and cut a piece of ¼-inch plywood to cover it. Round all the corners, treat it with wood preservative, and seal the edges with resin, just as you did for the seats.

Clamp the plywood onto the splash well so that it is flush with the top edge and just covers the bottom edge. Drill four evenly spaced ¼-inch holes through the plywood and the fiberglass behind. The ¼-inch hole will accept a ³/₁₆-inch wood nut, which in turn will accept a ¾-inch, 10-32 stainless machine screw. Remove the plywood and tap in the wood nuts from the front side, and you're ready to cover the ply.

Pick up a piece of ¾- or 1-inch-thick polyurethane foam and trim it so that it extends about ¼ inch beyond the edges of your plywood. Cover it with plastic, then a piece of matching upholstery, just as with the seats. Unless you want a two-color pattern, no special sewing is necessary; all you need is an extra bit of matching upholstery from the shop. If you want the two-tone pattern, the upholsterer probably has enough scraps left over from the seats to do the job. When you've got it covered and stapled, attach the panel by reaching under the splash well and inserting the machine screws into the wood nuts. Tighten them and you're done.

Improvements like this can be done with no special skills and very little extra cash. In this case, the improvement is probably cheaper than restoring the original—and far easier to maintain. Use your imagination. If there's something about your boat that you don't like, chances are you can rebuild it to suit. Coincidentally, that's the subject of the next chapter.

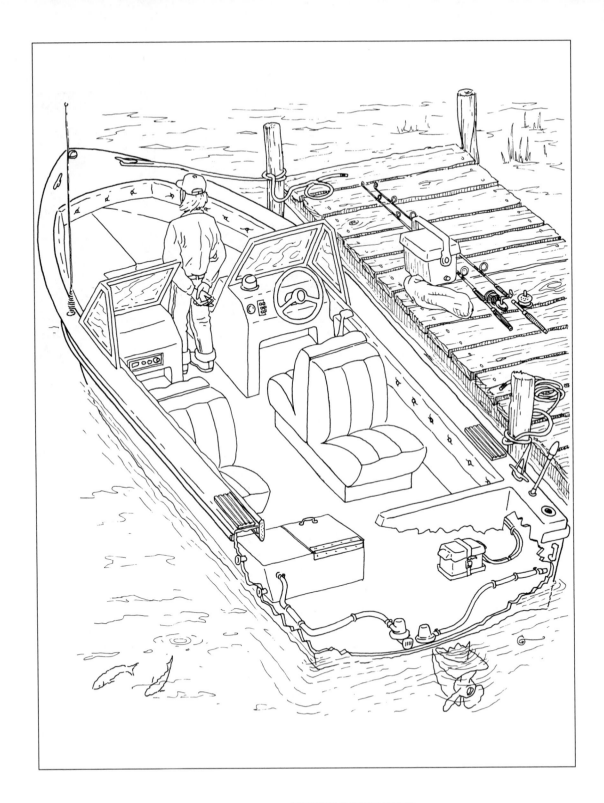

CHAPTER

8

Accessories, Improvements, and Tips

For those of you who have muscled your way through a fairly extensive renovation, some of the projects in this chapter will be finishing touches; others will be added bells and whistles that may not have been standard equipment when your boat was built. For those of you who have an older boat that just needs a little upgrading, this chapter may help you install an accessory or fix a problem that has been under your skin for awhile. And for all of you, I'll offer a few tips that will keep your new boat looking like new.

Keep Things Dry with a Bilge Pump

Few boats of this size and vintage included a bilge pump as standard equipment. The old solution to getting water out of the bilge was to take the boat out for a run at three-quarter throttle, crawl under the splash well, and pull the plug. It wasn't exactly elegant, but it served the purpose—as long as you had someone along to drive the boat.

I can't think of anyone who wouldn't find a bilge pump useful. If you're fishing in the rain, a bilge pump will keep you from having to make periodic bilge-clearing runs across the lake. The same goes if you kick over the cooler, or get caught in a little rough water. Perhaps the time you'll most appreciate a bilge pump is when you're sitting comfortably in the cabin playing cards while your boat sits out in the pouring rain. When it clears, you just stroll out and flip the switch.

Bilge pumps are rated by how many gallons per hour they'll pump, varying from around 300 to more than 2,000 g.p.h. You'd think that bigger is better. After all, if you have a 300-g.p.h. pump and 600 gallons of water in your boat, you probably don't want to know that it will take two hours to pump it all out—assuming the battery doesn't go flat (or short out underwater) in the interim. Large-capacity pumps use a great deal of electricity. The purpose of a bilge pump in boats of this size is to *conveniently* pump out the few gallons of water that inevitably accumulate in the bilge. If you've punched a big hole in your boat, better grab the minnow pail. A frightened person with a bucket can remove water faster than almost any mechanical device. For everyday use, you need a relatively moderate-capacity pump that will be easy on your battery.

For example, Attwood builds a 500-g.p.h. pump that draws less than one amp, recommended for boats up to 20 feet long, and a 360-g.p.h. pump recommended for boats under 17 feet. Depending on where you live and how you use your boat, either one of these two pumps, or similar ones from other manufacturers, should do just fine.

In addition to the pump, you'll have to buy a switch, a through-hull fitting, a few feet of bilge hose, two clamps, and perhaps some 18-gauge wire and connectors. You can purchase everything separately or in kit form. Mayfair, for instance, offers an installation kit for around $25.

Installing a bilge pump is pretty straightforward. Figure 8-1 shows the wiring and plumbing for a typical installation. Begin by locating a convenient spot for the switch, usually somewhere on the console. Most switches are mounted flush, which means you have to cut a hole in the console (usually backed with ³/₄-inch plywood) to accommodate it. Connect the wires to the switch, then mount it in the console. Run the two wires through the existing wiring harness aft to the battery, but don't connect them yet, and leave plenty of extra wire.

Next, you can install the through-hull fitting. If you've bought the parts separately, make sure that the fitting is the same size as the outlet on the pump. In most cases it will be ⁵/₈ or ³/₄ inch. The through hull should be mounted, as the name implies, through the side of the hull, and as high up as possible (make sure you can get to it from the inside). Usually, several inches below the rubrail and a foot forward of the transom is a good spot. If the inside access is uncommonly tight, you can use a 90-degree through hull, which will allow you to connect the hose from the bottom.

The shank of the fitting that goes through the hull normally will be ³/₄ or 1 inch in diameter. Drill the appropriate-size hole through the hull, put a good bead of silicone around the fitting's flange, and insert it from the outside. Go inside and screw on the plastic nut, but don't try to see how tight you can get it. It should be snug, with an even bead of silicone oozing out around the flange.

The pump should be located at the lowest point in the drain cavity, but be careful not to obstruct access to the drain plug. Also keep in mind

Figure 8-1. A vastly improved boat, showing a bilge-pump installation (lower right), a switch panel at the console, and a new live well (left).

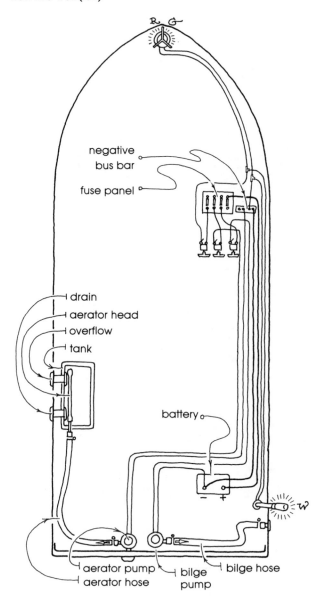

Figure 8-2. To install a bilge pump, you'll need a through-hull fitting. Mount it several inches below the rubrail and approximately a foot forward of the transom.

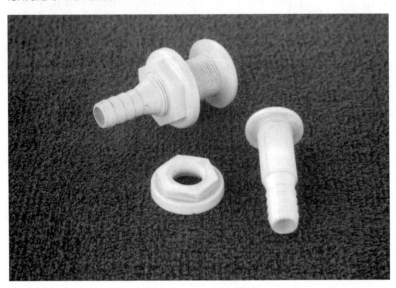

Figure 8-3. A bilge pump with a separate mounting bracket allows easy removal for cleaning.

that the pump's outlet must point in the general direction of the through-hull fitting, with enough room to attach the bilge hose without kinking.

The actual installation will depend on what pump you bought. Some have plastic flanges with predrilled mounting holes on the bottom. Others have a separate mounting bracket and strainer into which the pump itself snaps. This allows you to unsnap the pump and clean the strainer without removing the mounting screws. The pump should come with its own mounting screws, which are designed not to go through the bottom of your boat. If not, a 1/2-inch #8 stainless wood screw will hold the pump in place. When you've got the pump positioned where you want it, drill small pilot holes for each screw. Fill the pilot holes, using a good adhesive sealant instead of silicone, and screw the pump in place.

If you bought a kit, it probably came with bilge hose. If not, your marine store will have it in stock. You'll need enough so that you can push it up behind the splash well or somewhere where it won't be in the way of fuel tanks, batteries, etc. Attach one end to the through hull with a stainless hose clamp, run it to the pump, making sure it doesn't kink, and hook up the other end. (It doesn't really matter which end you hook up first; do whatever works best.)

The pump should come with a wiring diagram that tells which wire is hot and which is ground. Run the ground wire directly to the negative side of the battery. If you have to add a few feet of wire to make it reach, you can use crimped wireless connectors (seal each end with a dab of silicone).

Temporarily twist the hot wire to one of the wires from the switch. Twist the other wire from the switch to the positive terminal of the battery. Check out the pump and make sure that when the switch is "on," the pump is running. If the pump only runs when the switch is "off," reverse the two wires. It happens.

Installing a Live Well

We can probably thank the designers and builders of bassboats for the introduction of a relatively new but handy little accessory, the live well. The convenience of easily keeping your catch or bait alive caught on quickly; today, not just bassboats but all-purpose family boats like bow-riders are fitted with them. The components can be bought separately or in kit form. If you're a fisherman and your boat's design leaves you room to squeeze one in, you may want to install one.

A typical live-well system has three primary components: the pump, the aerator, and the tank assembly. Although the system may appear pretty basic, there are many things to consider before you make the decision to build one; some of you may have to accept the fact that it simply isn't practical for some boats.

The first thing you'll need to consider is where to locate the tank. Keep in mind that water weighs slightly more than 8 pounds per gallon.

Figure 8-4. A live-well installation. Ideally, the overflow and the drain will discharge directly through the hull.

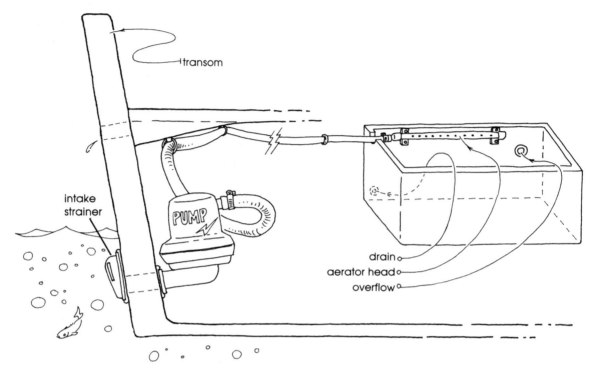

A cubic foot (12 inches by 12 inches by 12 inches) will hold 7.5 gallons of water, or approximately 60 pounds—a lot of weight to add to the extreme ends of your boat.

If you plan to use the live well for bait only, 3 or 4 gallons of water should be plenty, and the weight shouldn't be a factor in a typical 16-footer.

If you're planning to use the live well for fish, that could be a different matter. No live well is designed to hold large fish. You're better off knocking them on the head and throwing them on ice (don't ask me what ice weighs). Few factory-installed live wells in bassboats hold more than 10 to 12 gallons of water, but that's expected to hold a limit of bass. You're looking at an additional 80 pounds, though, which could affect how the boat handles and rides if it wasn't designed to handle it from the start.

If you have any question, grab your 80-pound kid (or the neighbor's) and take him for a boatride. Set him in those positions where you're thinking about placing your tank and see how it affects the boat's ride and handling. Keep in mind that you may be able to compensate for the additional weight by moving things like gas cans, batteries, and anchors.

Another consideration is the plumbing. Although there are any number of variations, all tanks must have an overflow and a drain, both of which have a definite impact on the tank's location. Ideally, both the overflow and the drain should be above the waterline, so that both can drain directly through the side of the hull using through-hull fittings and hose. To keep the hose lengths as short as possible, the tank should be positioned close to the hull.

Some boats plumb the overflow and the drain directly into the bilge, letting the bilge pump take care of the overflow, but I don't recommend this, particularly if you carry only a single battery. With the live-well pump drawing in fresh water and the bilge pump pumping it back out, your battery may be quickly discharged. Then too, your bilge may be too small to handle the live well's overflow (not to mention it will take on a decidedly fishy smell over time). The net result is, if you can't position the tank so that the overflow and the drain discharge through the hull, you may want to skip this project. You might as well throw a circulating pump in a 5-gallon pail.

In the flow-through system shown in Figure 8-4, a transom-mounted pump sprays a constant supply of fresh, oxygenated water into the tank through an aeration head. Mounting all the plumbing is fairly complicated, but with a constant supply of new, cool, fresh water, the fish or bait enjoys relative luxury as they await their fate. If this type of system is your choice, you'll have to plan for the supply hose—ideally before replacing the old floor. You can run the hose through the bilge or imbed it in the foam flotation.

The live-well pump is installed through a hole in the transom, to either side of the bilge drain below the waterline in the bilge cavity. If you already have a bilge pump in the cavity, you may not have room for another pump. But if you have the old floor out and you know that you want to install a bilge pump and a live-well pump, you can enlarge the drain cavity to suit.

Taking all this into consideration, you should now know if a live-well system will work in your boat. If you've decided to go ahead with the project, the next step is fabricating a tank.

The size of your tank will depend on your boat, intended use, and the tank's location, but there isn't much sense in building one that won't serve its intended purpose. If you only need to keep bait alive, the tank shouldn't need to hold more than a couple of gallons of water—at least twice that to hold a few fish. The top of the tank should extend several inches higher than the overflow outlet to keep water from splashing all over the boat.

I've built tanks of aluminum and wood. Either will work, but aluminum is much lighter and easier to install, and you never have to worry about rot. Unless you're a skilled tin-knocker, I suggest that you take your measurements to a local metal shop and have them bend the pieces to shape. If you want to pay the price, you can have them weld the parts together nice and watertight, or you can assemble them yourself using solid rivets and setting them as described in Appendix A, Renovating Aluminum Boats. When finished, you can paint or carpet the outside to match your interior. Aluminum definitely makes for a first-class live well, but it does get a little spendy, and you may opt for wood.

You may have enough scrap left over from the floor and transom to build a wood tank. Use 1/2-inch AC plywood; 1/4- or 3/8-inch ply is usually too flimsy to hold its shape. Cut the sides, ends, and bottom to your desired dimensions, leaving the finished side out, and treat the pieces with wood preservative.

When you're ready to assemble everything, coat all of the adjoining edges with resin, just as we did with the seat bases. Tack the pieces together with 6d galvanized finish nails. You just need to hold the box square and true until the resin cures and you can get the fiberglass on the inside.

When the resin cures, apply a bead of adhesive sealant such as Sikaflex to a piece of 1 × 2 and mount it around the inside top edge with 1-inch #8 stainless screws. This will serve as a mounting strip for a lid, or for hanging the live well under a bench seat.

Lay the tank on its side and cut a piece of mat that fits snugly under the 1 × 2 and extends onto the ends and bottom about 3 inches. Let it cure and repeat the process on the other side, both ends, and the bottom. Laying the tank flat and glassing each section separately is a little more time consuming than doing it all at a crack, but it eliminates the annoying tendency of mat and resin to sag when you rotate the box to cover a fresh area. Be free with the resin; use enough to cover the fibers of the mat completely.

If you want the inside colored, add fiberglass color pigment directly to the resin. Small bait such as minnows, fatheads, and shiners are hard to keep under the best conditions, and are extremely sensitive to toxins emitted by some paints. Besides, if the color is locked right in the resin, you'll never have to repaint. You can finish the outside of the tank with paint or carpet. If the tank is doubling as a seat, add a lid with a brass or stainless piano hinge, a cushion, and matching upholstery.

Now you've got some plumbing to do. Figure 8-4 shows two sides of a typical tank with the necessary fittings in place. The fittings are installed just the same as the through hull for the bilge pump, but there are a couple of tips. The through-hull fitting for the drain should be at least 1 inch (inside diameter) so that it will drain quickly and accept the same type of drain plug that's in the bilge drain (if you've ever launched your boat without putting in the plug, you'll appreciate why it's handy to have a same-size spare close at hand). The overflow should be at least 1½ inches I.D. to allow free flow. You can buy bilge hose this size, but a piece of radiator hose will serve as well.

Because most boats sit a little bow high, the drain should be located on the aft side of the tank. Set the tank in place before you cut any holes to ensure that there is a slight slope from the tank fittings to the through hulls.

When you cut the hole through the transom for the pump, make sure it's perpendicular to the angle of the transom. Most kits come with anti-airlock shims designed to compensate for the angle of the transom; these keep the pump level and prevent air locks. After you figure out that, just mount the pump following the same procedure that you used for the bilge pump's through-hull fitting. Cut off the excess intake tube with a hacksaw. You may want to add a strainer over the pump intake to keep grass and muck from plugging the pump or getting to the aerator head.

There. That should do it.

Don't Be Afraid of the Dark

I don't know of anything on a small boat that gives me a headache quicker than lights that don't work—or worse, those that only work when they feel like it. Most boats already have lights, so I won't discuss installation. But if you're renovating an old runabout, now's the time to take care of lighting problems, *before* you stay out late fishing and find your running lights don't work.

The first thing most of us do when we notice a light that isn't working is check the bulb. Because it's easy, I suppose it's a good place to start, but be honest: How many bad 12-volt bulbs have you found?

Most boats of this size have a bow light and a stern light. The bow light, which is usually securely mounted, well sealed, and has wiring protected from the elements, seldom causes problems. If a bow light doesn't work, the problem may very well be the bulb. If it isn't, check the switch.

One of the most common switches used in boats of this era (and today) was a three-position, push-pull switch. When the switch is all the way in, it's "off." Pull it out one position, and the bow light comes on; all the way out, and both the bow and stern lights come on. Or at least that's the plan.

I can't begin to count how many of those switches I've replaced over the years. After the second one went bad on my own boat I decided that there had to be a better way. I threw it in the junk pile and wired the bow light and the stern light to their own all-weather toggle switches. The two switches cost only slightly more than the three-position switch; I haven't had a problem since.

The next problem, and one that seems almost unsolvable, is the stern light itself. Many states mandate how high above the deck the stern light must be—some as much as 48 inches high. Because these won't fit under your boat cover and are always in the way, companies like Attwood and Perko have tried to solve the problem with stowaway telescoping light poles, or removable lights that plug into a permanently mounted base.

Unfortunately, none of them have been completely successful in eliminating the problems, nor have I. I do have a couple of suggestions, though.

If you've got a telescoping stern light, one of those where you loosen a nut at the base and push the light down, do it and see what happens to the wires coming out of the bottom of the tube. They're probably pinched between the tube and the floor; if you check, I doubt that you'll find any type of grommet or protection to keep the wires from chafing on the tube. Pull the tube all the way out. With one hand, center the wires so that they don't touch the tube. With the other hand, fill the end of the tube with silicone and let it set up. That will prevent your wires from getting chafed, pinched, or cut off for many years.

At the other end you'll find a plastic dome that covers the bulb. Check it for cracks and replace it if necessary. If you screw off the dome you'll see that it's sealed with a rubber or cork gasket. Check these periodically. If they're brittle or broken, replace them. It'll help to keep water out of the socket and minimize corrosion. Perko and Attwood (probably the largest suppliers of lights) both make replacement domes and gaskets. If your marine dealer doesn't have them in stock, he can order them.

If you've got a stern light that plugs into a deck-mounted socket, spray the male and female contacts with contact cleaner (check Radio Shack) on occasion. Better yet, keep a can in the boat. It may prove to be a quick fix some dark and stormy night.

Beyond these few tips I can only suggest that you learn where to look for problems and practice a little preventive maintenance.

Eliminate the Bird's Nest

We've added a bilge pump, maybe a live-well pump, and a toggle switch for the lighting system. Throw in an AM/FM radio, a couple of fish finders, a horn, and a spotlight, and what have you got? In most cases, you've got a terrific bird's nest of wires stuffed under the splash well and wrapped around the battery.

The electrical systems in boats of this vintage were pretty basic. There were few, if any, instruments and only a few lights. If there was an accessory that required fusing it was usually supplied with an in-line fuse holder.

It's not my intent to go into a lengthy technical discussion on 12-volt wiring systems. There are simply too many good, comprehensive books (like *The 12-Volt Bible for Boats*, Seven Seas Press, 1985) available that discuss ohms and watts and volts and amps, as well as the installation of specific accessories. But you've invested substantial time and cash in renovating your boat. The job isn't finished until the electrical system is also upgraded, and the first step in upgrading is to eliminate the bird's nest.

Figure 8-5 shows the best antidote, a console-mounted gang switch panel. The switches and fuses are always at your fingertips, and there is no bird's nest at the battery. A properly installed system such as this will nearly eliminate chafed and broken wires and the associated headaches. These console-mounted panels are usually expensive ($25 and up), but well worth the investment.

If you're pinching pennies, there is a cheaper option: a DC distribution panel and a negative buss bar mounted under the console. Combined, they serve substantially the same purpose as the switch panel, and

Figure 8-5. Installing a console-mounted gang switch panel should be your first step when upgrading the electrical system.

Figure 8-6. A 12-volt distribution system like this will tame the usual bird's nest of unknown wires that lurks beneath the console.

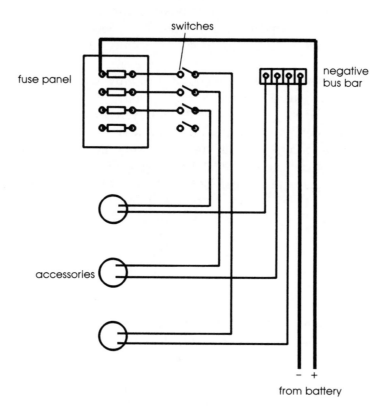

they are much cheaper. Access is still easy, and the bird's nest is eliminated. Fusing of individual accessories is accomplished at the DC distribution panel.

Again, if you're not familiar with basic DC electricity, I suggest that you pick up a good book and study it. That knowledge combined with the wiring instructions for your specific accessories will make the job easy. And you'll never again trip over a bird's nest of wires in the back of your boat.

Mounting Hardware

Most people seem to enter a boat from the dock in one of two ways: Either they first step on the seat (and your new upholstery), and then into the boat; or they step on the gunnel (and your new paint). A couple of

Figure 8-7. Add step pads to protect your newly renovated runabout's pristine finish from the menace of incautious feet.

inexpensive step pads and a stern captain who isn't afraid to tell people where to step will take the heat off both your upholstery and paint.

You should be able to find step pads, in a variety of sizes and materials, at any well-stocked marine store.

Installation is simple. Most frames are predrilled to accommodate #10 stainless sheetmetal screws. Just position the pads where they're most needed, drill through the top of the gunnel, screw them in place, and you're done—or at least so the instructions say.

But this is where I stray from common practice. Long ago I established a rule that says whenever I mount deck hardware, I add a backing plate under it. I also use machine screws in place of wood- or sheetmetal screws.

Many builders glassed in a piece of ³/₈- or ¹/₂-inch plywood on the underside of the gunnel for additional support and to help distribute pressure on the deck hardware. Many didn't, though, and if it isn't there the top of the gunnel is pretty thin to support someone's weight.

Because step pads aren't usually subjected to a lot of lateral stress, the backing plate can be most anything. A scrap piece of plywood treated with wood preservative will work well. Simply cut it the width of the pad, drill matching holes, and bolt the pad and the backer together, with the gunnel sandwiched between, using stainless machine screws.

If you look around, you'll find many cleats with hairline gelcoat cracks extending out from the corners of the cleat. Often, that results from stress because of the lack of an adequate backing plate. A cleat mounted on the top of the gunnel is subject to a lot of lateral strain from docklines. When mounting cleats I usually add a piece of $1/8$ inch aluminum on the bottom side to spread the strain.

Again, there may already be plywood on the underside of the gunnel, and if it's in good condition, that's all you need. In either case I suggest that you use a machine screw with flat washers and self-locking nuts on the bottom side. They are less likely to work loose and damage the fiberglass. Remember, any time you drill through plywood, you must seal the holes with bedding compound.

Which brings me to a short discussion on bedding compounds, sealants, and adhesives. Throughout the book I have suggested using products such as 3M-5200, Sikaflex, or silicone depending on the application. Technically, none of these products can be defined as bedding compounds. From a practical standpoint, these space-age products serve the same functions as old-fashioned bedding compound, and work much better. To me, they've all become bedding compounds.

When mounting deck hardware such as the cleat above, we need not be concerned with using a product that has superior adhesion qualities such as 3M-5200 or Sikaflex. We're using machine screws to make sure they stay in place. A good sealant such as silicone will keep water from dripping into the boat or reaching a plywood backing for many years.

Many builders of older boats didn't use a bedding compound or sealant under deck hardware (can you say planned obsolescence?), but I think it's a good idea. Check your cleats, step pads, and light bases. If they're dripping a little, remove them, clean the deck, and add a bead of silicone around the base.

If you add a bracket to the top of your console for a fish finder, a dab of silicone in the screw holes might prevent water from reaching electrical connections on the back side of the console.

When adding transom accessories, such as a transducer or pitot tube for a speedometer, which will be subjected to more abuse, you might want to use one of the adhesives. Regardless of what you choose, this is one place where you want to seal the water away from your new transom.

In short, take a close look at all of your existing hardware and take care when mounting accessories. When possible, use stainless machine screws as opposed to sheetmetal screws and make sure that they are properly sealed.

If your boat was built in the 1950s or early 1960s, you may have one of the last cable-and-pulley steering systems around. They may be unsightly and a little sloppy at the wheel, but they did the job for many years. However, a single-cable steering system eliminates the annoying rattle of cable-and-pulley systems, and is so much more responsive that you may want to modernize. If you're thinking of converting to a modern control head and cable assembly, plan on spending about $250 for the whole setup—a wheel, bezel, control head, cable assembly, and motor connectors.

I'm not going to detail a conversion here. For one thing, there is no such thing as a "typical" conversion. Each boat is different, each brand of mechanical steering is different, and each installs differently to different brands of motors. If you are one of the few who still has a cable-and-pulley system, and you feel the need to convert, I suggest that you sit down with a good mechanic and let him help you design a system that will work for your boat and engine.

It's far more likely that your boat already has a mechanical steering system; if it's a couple of decades old, it will probably need some rebuilding—especially if you bought an older boat that has been sitting out, unprotected, in the grove.

A mechanical steering system has five basic parts, but only two account for the majority of the problems: the cable and the control head. Naturally, they are the most expensive parts to replace.

Identifying the problem is fairly easy: If your steering system is okay, you'll be able to swing the wheel easily with one hand. If the wheel turns steadily but is very stiff, the problem is likely the cable. If the wheel jams or jerks during the sweep, check the control head.

In either case, your repair options are a bit limited. If you have a bad cable, there is only one thing you can try before replacing it. This rarely works, because most cables are completely sealed at the ends, but it's worth a try. Figure 8-8 shows the steering-cable hookup at the engine. Clean the stainless pushrod at the motor end with degreaser and lubricate it with a light grease. Swing the wheel several times and see if it loosens up. It didn't? Then you need a new cable.

Disconnecting the cable at the motor end is simple. Just remove the bolt that fastens the control rod to the end of the cable. The other end is a little more tricky.

To change the cable *and* service the control head, you'll have to re-

Figure 8-8. Before you decide to replace the steering cable, clean and lubricate the pushrod near the motor, then work the wheel a bit. It just may loosen up.

move the head from the console. Pop out the plastic plate in the center of the steering wheel, then remove the screws or nut that holds the wheel to the plastic bezel. You'll see a couple more screws that attach the bezel to the console or the control head itself. Pull those, then remove the bezel.

The wheel shaft will probably be attached to the bracket with a single nut. When you remove the nut, the control head will be free. The precise method of mounting will depend on the type and brand of control head, but Figure 8-10 shows a typical setup. There are several manufacturers of steering systems—Teleflex, Morse, DetMar, and Acco Babcock to name a few. They are all different in detail, yet all can be classified into two basic designs. The first is often referred to as the *rack*, or the rack-and-pinion head—in my opinion, the most positive and trouble-free system available. The wheel shaft is attached to a round gear in the head, which is in turn geared to the rack pressed onto the end of the steering cable. As you turn the wheel the ring gear drives the rack to the left or right.

The other basic design is the *rotary head* (Figure 8-11). Figure 8-10 shows its basic configuration. A rotary-head system uses a coiled stainless steel, kind of like the Roto-Rooter you use to clean your drains, which sets into a matching, grooved, gear-driven hub. As you turn the wheel, the ca-

Figure 8-9. To change the cable and service the control head, pop out the plastic piece in the center of the wheel; the nut that holds the wheel on is behind it.

Figure 8-10. This is a common method of mounting the control head and wheel. With a rotary-head steering system, as the wheel turns, the cable is drawn through the inlet, around the drum, and out the take-up tube. A rack-and-pinion system moves the rack-and-cable assembly from side to side.

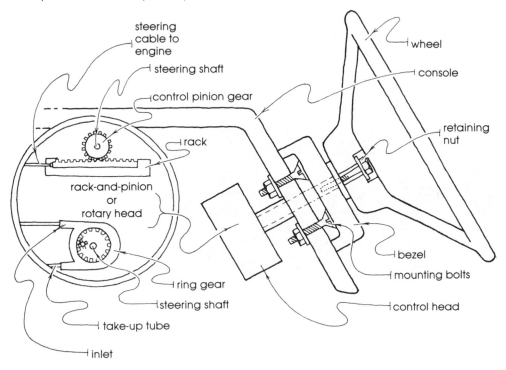

ble coils up in a circle inside the head. The dotted lines in Figure 8-10 represent a variation of the rotary head. In this design, the used cable makes a single pass around the hub and into a piece of plastic called a *spent tube*.

Regardless of what type you have, if you are having steering problems, I suggest that you take the unit apart, clean it up, and regrease it. Don't be afraid to take it apart. There aren't any giant springs that will jump out and bite you, and from a mechanical standpoint, they're pretty straightforward. A rotary head can run as much as $100 without the cable, and a rack with cable as much as $225. A little maintenance will be well worth your time.

Keep Her Lookin' Good

I don't think it's any secret that a boat belonging to a meticulous owner—someone who is always waxing and polishing and cleaning—will last much longer than a boat belonging to someone completely indifferent to maintenance. Regardless of where you fall between those two extremes, there are a few easy and inexpensive things you can do to prolong the life of your newly renovated runabout.

Tarps and Canvas

Recent years have not been kind to many segments of the marine industry. New-boat sales are down in many parts of the country on nearly every size of boat. It isn't that fewer people are going boating—far from it. It's just that in today's economy, people tend to hang on to what they

Figure 8-11. A typical rotary-head steering system.

have. Perhaps it's that trend that accounts for the prosperity of the marine canvas business. There are few investments that will do more to extend a boat's lifespan than a good tarp.

In most parts of the country, a new custom tarp for a typical 16-foot boat can be bought for around $200 (storebought tarps start around $100). When you stop to consider how much you just invested in floor covering, paint, and upholstery, that's a small price to pay to protect your renovated runabout from the elements. Rain and snow may cause problems with rot, but your boat's true enemy, at least cosmetically speaking, is the sun. Those of you who live in south Florida are all too familiar with this. But even in the Great White North boats suffer under the hot summer sun.

Like most things, there are good tarps and bad tarps. Here are a few tips that will help you acquire a good one. First and foremost, I suggest that you have a tarp custom-built as opposed to buying a one-size-fits-all tarp off the shelf. You'll probably spend a little extra, but you can have it tailored to fit your own engine (Will a tarp designed to fit either a towering in-line six Mercury or a squat V-4 Johnson really fit either one?) and any other hardware—windshields, consoles, lights—that sticks up above deck level. You'll also have some control over the weight and type of material, and you can add a few extras that aren't usually standard on store-bought tarps.

If you order a custom tarp from an average shop without specifying the material, you'll probably get a brand of preshrunk cotton marine canvas. When wet, the fibers shrink and it becomes watertight. When dry it breathes well, which eliminates condensation. Marine canvas can be purchased in a variety of weights ranging from 10 to 24 ounces per square yard, which allows you to make the decision on how much you want to spend compared with how much abuse the tarp is likely to suffer.

Although there are several others, a second *practical* choice in material is one made of acrylic fibers. These materials will far outlast cotton, but are more expensive, only available in a single weight, and are considered water resistant instead of waterproof. Because it breathes it will minimize condensation, but it will also allow a bit of water to seep into the boat. It's also susceptible to chafe, which means that problem areas will need to be reinforced with leather, Dacron, or another suitable product. Of course that's a good idea anyway, with any material.

In fact, it's one of the primary advantages of having a tarp custom built. Stern caps, the bow cap, and the corners of a windshield should be reinforced as well as any other piece of hardware that may subject the tarp to excessive wear.

Figure 8-12. A flap under the tie-down eye will prevent the lines that secure the tarp from scratching the paint.

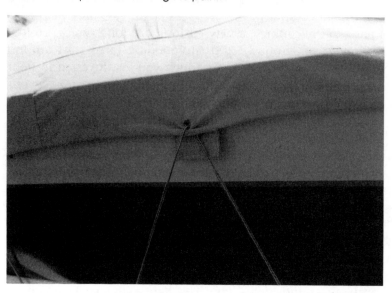

Here's another of the details that separates a shelf tarp from a custom one: See the flap under the tie-down eye on the tarp in Figure 8-12? Without that flap, the first time you tie down a tarp your flawless new paint job is scratched. And if your tie-down lines run under the boat and tie off on the trailer, you can further protect your paint by covering each line with a foam sleeve. Puritan makes one intended for use on sailboat lifelines or shrouds. They work equally well to pad your tie-down lines.

A well-designed custom tarp shouldn't need any additional support underneath to shed water properly. Generally, the windshield and seats will help to give it a proper slope so water will run off. But if you've got an older tarp, it may sag in the middle, which allows water to form a puddle—which usually ends up in the boat.

The problem can be solved by adding one or two strategically placed support bows. These can be bought in either fiberglass or oak (I prefer oak), and come with two chrome fittings that mount on opposite sides of the vertical side of the gunnel. Be sure to use machine screws and a small backing plate to attach them; they'll take some abuse in a good wind. Cut the bows to a length that gives the tarp a good crown to ensure the water runs off quickly.

Of course a tarp doesn't protect your boat very effectively folded up in the garage. Try to develop the habit of putting it on every time you put the boat away, particularly if you keep it in a slip or store it in the backyard. But there's no denying that a full-cover tarp can be a pain to put on and take off if you're using the boat every day. If you're on a two-week vacation with your boat at the dock, you probably won't bother to put it on after each use. I know I wouldn't.

Fortunately there's an interim alternative for lazy folks like us. The same shop that builds the tarp can fashion lightweight, easily stowed covers for lounge or pedestal seats, fish finders, engines, compasses, or other accessories that you want to protect from the sun. It only takes a few minutes each evening to throw them on. And it sure beats reupholstering your renovated runabout a few years down the road.

What's a Boat Fender?

Some of you may scoff because I'm devoting a couple of paragraphs to the use of boat fenders, or bumpers, to some. Let me assure you: A large segment of small-boat owners don't know what boat fenders are. Those people kept me in business. The prevailing mentality seems to be that fenders only serve a useful purpose on "big" boats. But try this: Take a good look at your new paint job, reflecting on the hours of labor that went into it, then go take a good look at a typical boat dock.

Depending on the shape of the hull, the average 16-foot boat needs no more than two 4- by 16-inch fenders to protect it from most docks. Pick them up at any marine store for around $10 each; tie on a few feet of nylon utility line, and get in the habit of dropping them over the side as you approach the dock.

Once tied up, spend a few minutes adjusting your dock lines and the height of the fenders. I usually stand around for a few minutes and check out the wave or wake action to make sure that the fenders are positioned properly. The alternative is another spell of sanding and painting. No thanks.

One caution: Don't leave the things hanging over the side when you're out running around the lake. True mariners think this looks tacky; they'll laugh and point at you.

Don't Ignore Your Trailer

Figure 8-13 shows a damaged bow—a type of damage that's all too common, and so easily avoided. If this boat's owner had spent 10 minutes adjusting the bracket that mounts the rubber "V" stop, he could have avoided that ding. In most cases, it's a simple matter of loosening a single bolt and adjusting the angle of the bracket.

If the rubber "V" is hard and brittle or missing, replace it. The same applies to the rollers. Over time they become very hard; if the boat is stored on the trailer, its weight will eventually flatten them in spots. The result is scratches and dents on the boat's bottom. Unfortunately, trailer

Figure 8-13. Don't let this happen to your boat. Adjust the angle of the bracket to prevent the trailer from damaging the bow.

rollers are expensive to replace (you may have as many as 16 of them, at up to $12 a pop), but I still recommend that you do it every few years. Painting ain't cheap either.

Summary

That pretty much covers the most common upgrades and improvements that I have been asked to do over the years. I didn't get them all, of course. There are fish finders, horns (my eyes are rolling), speedometers, flag staffs, radios, and a dozen others. Most accessories such as fish finders and speedometers come with detailed installation instructions, and I simply can't cover all the possible additions.

My intent was to provide an overall approach to adding accessories and upgrades and to offer a few tips on keeping your renovation looking good for a few extra years. If you want to go beyond that, you're only limited by your wallet and your imagination.

Renovating Aluminum Boats

An Old Debate

For those of you who bought this book to help you decide on a good used boat, I feel obliged to tell you that aluminum is not my favorite boatbuilding material. I don't care for the way aluminum boats ride or handle; I don't care for the odd noises they make—especially after a box of split-shot sinkers finds its way into the bilge; and I don't care for the way they heat up in the sun and blister your behind.

For the average guy, aluminum boats are also difficult and expensive to repair; in many cases, there simply *is* no repair. A relatively minor mishap with a fiberglass boat can be repaired quickly and cheaply. The same mishap with an aluminum boat may mean it's totaled, paving the way for an unpleasant experience with your insurance agent.

I have restored and repaired many aluminum boats. When painting or replacing a floor, they are much cleaner to work on than fiberglass boats, but if you develop a leak (and sooner or later you will) you've usually got serious problems.

Like fiberglass boats, there are good and bad aluminum boats. A guy brought me a Sylvan one day to see what I could do. Although it was less than a year old, more than half of the rivets had come loose below the waterline. I helped him contact the factory (who to their credit made good on the repair), but it illustrates the problem. Over the years I had a steady stream of aluminum boats of all makes coming into my shop with loose rivets and leaks. Unless you're prepared to spend $600 to $800 on a blind-rivet gun, the only way to repair them properly is to remove the floor.

Their primary selling point has always been that they weigh considerably less than a fiberglass boat of the same size. True, but when you consider that weight (or displacement) is directly related to safety and comfort, I'll stick with the heavier boat. I'm also convinced that the light weight is partially responsible for the problem of loose rivets.

In their favor I should say that their light weight makes them somewhat more fuel efficient. And I've never seen an aluminum boat with a rotten transom; theirs are protected and ventilated far better than most fiberglass boats.

Aluminum boatbuilders are still progressing, though, just as the builders of fiberglass boats did in the 1950s and 1960s. Crestliner now welds the bow stem and keel on their boats—a considerable improvement over rivets. Fisher now builds a line of boats with aluminum floors, which certainly solves the rot problem, and further lightens the boat to boot.

The debate—aluminum or fiberglass—will go on forever.

Replacing the Floor and Stopping the Leaks

For those of you who own an older aluminum boat with a rotten floor, or are thinking about buying one, you're faced with many of the same problems as the guy next door with a fiberglass boat.

As with the fiberglass boat, seats and other interior accessories are attached to the floor with stainless sheetmetal screws. Removal is a piece of cake (see Chapter 4).

Once you've removed the seats and accessories, take up whatever floor covering you may have. You'll immediately notice the difference between fiberglass and aluminum. The floor is attached to aluminum frames and stringers with aluminum pop rivets, usually $3/16$ by $3/4$ inch, although the size may vary depending on the builder. Start with a $3/16$ bit and drill out a couple until you determine the actual diameter. Once you're sure of the size, simply drill out every rivet you can find in the floor. It'll fall out.

Once the floor is out, you'll be faced with the flotation problems described in Chapter 4. Again, don't waste time with it. If it's wet, throw it away and replace it.

Obviously, because the stringers and frames are made of aluminum, you don't need to worry about replacing them. However, at this stage, there is an extra step that I recommend to anyone who has invested the effort to remove the floor in their aluminum boat: Check the hull for leaks.

Make sure that the boat is sitting level on the trailer (or blocks). Fill it with water to floor level and let it sit for a couple of hours. Then inspect each rivet, *without crawling under the boat*, which is a little heavy at this point. Should it fall, you'd get squashed. You'll quickly spot any leakers; mark them with a permanent marking pen and drain the water.

Unlike the rivets used in the floor, those in the hull are solid aluminum, for obvious reasons. They may range in size from $1/8$ inch to $1/4$ inch in the same boat, depending on its size, builder, and application. I suggest that you start with a $1/8$-inch drill bit until you determine the rivets' size.

From the outside, set a small dent in the head of the rivet with a center punch to keep your bit from wandering. Drill it out and check to see if any of the rivet remains in the hole. If it does, your bit is too small; move up a size.

Once you've determined the size of the rivets, move up another size and drill out all of the leakers. A rivet that has been loose for any length of time has wobbled in the hole and probably enlarged the original hole. To ensure a tight seal, you'll need to replace the leakers with a rivet a size larger.

The length of the rivets will vary depending on where they are used. Usually, frames are a bit thicker than the hull material. The new rivet should be about $3/16$ to $1/4$ inch longer than the thickness of the two pieces of material. If you're a poor guesser on the length, it may take a couple of trips to the hardware store to get what you need.

Clean the hull around the holes (inside and out) with acetone or a degreaser. Because you set the rivets by hand, I suggest that you also seal them with a good sealant like 3M-5200 or Sikaflex. Now you'll need to round up a little help.

Apply a dab of sealant to the hole and insert the rivets from the outside. Have your helper hold the rivet in place with a heavy hammer or a large piece of metal (the base of a small hydraulic jack works well). From the inside, flatten the rivet shank and round it over with a ballpeen hammer until the head of the rivet has drawn up tight on the outside. Your leak is fixed.

When you're satisfied with the leak repair job, you're ready to install the new floor. Again, use AC-grade plywood, cut and fitted just as on the fiberglass boat (see Chapter 4). Because the new floor won't have a fiberglass coating, you'll have to coat both sides with a good wood preservative. If you want to spend the money, there is another preventive measure that will ensure the life of the wood.

We've been using polyester resin for all repairs, simply because it's cheap and that's what the builders used originally. For this application, though, we can saturate the new floor pieces with epoxy resin. Epoxy resin cures much, much more slowly than polyester. Consequently, it tends to saturate the plywood to a greater extent. Once cured, the floor is nearly indestructible. Epoxy resin isn't cheap, though. If you're buying polyester resin for $16 to $20 at discount (a fairly average price), figure on paying $70 a gallon for epoxy at the same outlet. But, because you won't use as much resin and there's no fiberglass cloth or mat involved, the final cost may be close to the same as that for the fiberglass floor.

When you have the new floor pieces cut and treated, they're ready to put down. Hit as many of the original holes in the stringers and frames as you can, but don't worry if you miss a few; simply drill new holes when necessary. Because these rivets may be ¾ inch long, snapping them off with a hand-operated pop-rivet gun is no easy task. By the time the last one is in, you may have trouble picking up a coffee cup.

When the new floor is in place, cover it with carpet as we did in Chapter 4. Reattach all the seats and interior accessories with stainless sheet-metal screws, and remember to use a good sealant.

There. You've got a new floor.

APPENDIX

B

Suppliers

I won't try to list the names and addresses of every manufacturer and wholesaler of marine products. The list is nearly endless. If your local marine dealer doesn't have what you need, pick up any popular boating magazine and read the ads. Most big mail-order companies like West Marine Products, Defender Industries, or EBI offer catalogs free or for a few bucks.

The companies listed here are harder to find, and a bit more specialized. LBI is a wholesaler and retailer specializing in fiberglass products, resins, sealants, coatings, fastenings, a variety of safety products, supplies, and tools. They also offer technical support.

Wefco claims to be the largest U.S. manufacturer of replacement rubrails—new or old. They also make window rubbers, dock bumpers, windshield rubber, and many other hard-to-find items.

Jamestown and Hamilton Marine both offer a good selection of stainless fasteners and boatbuilding materials.

I highly recommend all these companies. Give them a call for a catalog.

LBI, Inc.
973 North Road (Route 117)
Groton, CT 06340
(800) 231-6537

Wefco Rubber Manufacturing
  Company
1655 Euclid Street
Santa Monica, CA 90404-3772
(213) 393-0303 or 0304

Jamestown Distributors
28 Narragansett Avenue
P.O. Box 348
Jamestown, RI 02835
(401) 423-2520

Hamilton Marine
155 East Main Street
Searsport, ME 04974
(207) 548-6302

Index